Betty Friedan

Betty Friedan

JUSTINE BLAU

CHELSEA HOUSE PUBLISHERS

NEW YORK · PHILADELPHIA

Chelsea House Publishers
EDITOR-IN-CHIEF Remmel Nunn
MANAGING EDITOR Karyn Gullen Browne
COPY CHIEF Juliann Barbato
PICTURE EDITOR Adrian G. Allen
ART DIRECTOR Maria Epes
DEPUTY COPY CHIEF Mark Rifkin
ASSISTANT ART DIRECTOR Loraine Machlin
MANUFACTURING MANAGER Gerald Levine
SYSTEMS MANAGER Rachel Vigier
PRODUCTION MANAGER Joseph Romano
PRODUCTION COORDINATOR Marie Claire Cebrián

American Women of Achievement
SENIOR EDITOR Richard Rennert

Staff for BETTY FRIEDAN
TEXT EDITOR Ellen Scordato
COPY EDITOR Philip Koslow
EDITORIAL ASSISTANT Nicole Claro
PICTURE RESEARCHER Michèle Brisson
DESIGN ASSISTANT Debora Smith
COVER ILLUSTRATOR Daniel Mark Duffy

First Printing

1 3 5 7 9 8 6 4 2

Library of Congress Cataloging-in-Publication Data

Blau, Justine.
  Betty Friedan/by Justine Blau.
    p.   cm.—(American women of achievement)
  Includes bibliographical references
  Summary: A biography of the author of *The Feminine Mys-
tique* who helped found the National Organization for Women
in 1966.
ISBN 1-55546-653-2
     0-7910-0433-3 (pbk.)
  1. Friedan, Betty—Juvenile literature.   2. Feminists—
United States—Biography—Juvenile literature.   3.
Feminism—United States—Juvenile literature. [1. Friedan,
Betty. 2. Feminists.] I. Title. II. Series
HQ1413.F75B57 1990
305.42′0973′092—dc20   89-77027
[B]   CIP
[92]   AC

398716

CONTENTS

AMERICAN WOMEN OF ACHIEVEMENT

Abigail Adams
women's rights advocate

Jane Addams
social worker

Louisa May Alcott
author

Marian Anderson
singer

Susan B. Anthony
woman suffragist

Ethel Barrymore
actress

Clara Barton
founder of the American Red Cross

Elizabeth Blackwell
physician

Nellie Bly
journalist

Margaret Bourke-White
photographer

Pearl Buck
author

Rachel Carson
biologist and author

Mary Cassatt
artist

Agnes de Mille
choreographer

Emily Dickinson
poet

Isadora Duncan
dancer

Amelia Earhart
aviator

Mary Baker Eddy
founder of the Christian Science church

Betty Friedan
feminist

Althea Gibson
tennis champion

Emma Goldman
political activist

Helen Hayes
actress

Lillian Hellman
playwright

Katharine Hepburn
actress

Karen Horney
psychoanalyst

Anne Hutchinson
religious leader

Mahalia Jackson
gospel singer

Helen Keller
humanitarian

Jeane Kirkpatrick
diplomat

Emma Lazarus
poet

Clare Boothe Luce
author and diplomat

Barbara McClintock
biologist

Margaret Mead
anthropologist

Edna St. Vincent Millay
poet

Julia Morgan
architect

Grandma Moses
painter

Louise Nevelson
sculptor

Sandra Day O'Connor
Supreme Court justice

Georgia O'Keeffe
painter

Eleanor Roosevelt
diplomat and humanitarian

Wilma Rudolph
champion athlete

Florence Sabin
medical researcher

Beverly Sills
opera singer

Gertrude Stein
author

Gloria Steinem
feminist

Harriet Beecher Stowe
author and abolitionist

Mae West
entertainer

Edith Wharton
author

Phillis Wheatley
poet

Babe Didrikson Zaharias
champion athlete

CHELSEA HOUSE PUBLISHERS

"REMEMBER THE LADIES"

MATINA S. HORNER

Remember the Ladies." That is what Abigail Adams wrote to her husband, John, then a delegate to the Continental Congress, as the Founding Fathers met in Philadelphia to form a new nation in March of 1776. "Be more generous and favorable to them than your ancestors. Do not put such unlimited power in the hands of the Husbands. If particular care and attention is not paid to the Ladies," Abigail Adams warned, "we are determined to foment a Rebellion, and will not hold ourselves bound by any Laws in which we have no voice, or Representation."

The words of Abigail Adams, one of the earliest American advocates of women's rights, were prophetic. Because when we have not "remembered the ladies," they have, by their words and deeds, reminded us so forcefully of the omission that we cannot fail to remember them. For the history of American women is as interesting and varied as the history of our nation as a whole. American women have played an integral part in founding, settling, and building our country. Some we remember as remarkable women who—against great odds—achieved distinction in the public arena: Anne Hutchinson, who in the 17th century became a charismatic religious leader; Phillis Wheatley, an 18th-century black slave who became a poet; Susan B. Anthony, whose name is synonymous with the 19th-century women's rights movement and who led the struggle to enfranchise women; and, in our own century, Amelia Earhart, the first woman to cross the Atlantic Ocean by air.

These extraordinary women certainly merit our admiration, but other women, "common women," many of them all but forgotten, should also be recognized for their contributions to American thought and culture. Women have been community builders; they have founded schools and formed voluntary associations to help those in need; they have assumed the major responsibility for rearing children, passing on from one generation to the next the values that keep a culture alive. These and innumerable other contributions, once ignored, are now being recognized by scholars, students, and the public. It is exciting and gratifying to realize that a part of our history that was hardly acknowledged a few generations ago is now being studied and brought to light.

In recent decades, the field of women's history has grown from obscurity to a politically controversial splinter movement to academic respectability, in many cases mainstreamed into such traditional disciplines as history, economics, and psychology. Scholars of women, both female and male, have organized research centers at such prestigious institutions as Wellesley College, Stanford University, and the University of California. Other notable centers for women's studies are the Center for the American Woman and Politics at the Eagleton Institute of Politics at Rutgers University; the Henry A. Murray Research Center for the Study of Lives, at Radcliffe College; and the Women's Research and Education Institute, the research arm of the Congressional Caucus on Women's Issues. Other scholars and public figures have established archives and libraries, such as the Schlesinger Library on the History of Women in America, at Radcliffe College, and the Sophia Smith Collection, at Smith College, to collect and preserve the written and tangible legacies of women.

From the initial donation of the Women's Rights Collection in 1943, the Schlesinger Library grew to encompass vast collections documenting the manifold accomplishments of American women. Simultaneously, the women's movement in general and the academic discipline of women's studies in particular also began with a narrow definition and gradually expanded their mandate. Early causes such as woman suffrage and social reform, abolition and organized labor were joined by newer concerns such as the history of women in business and the professions and in politics and government; the study of the family; and social issues such as health policy and education.

Women, as historian Arthur M. Schlesinger, jr., once pointed out, "have constituted the most spectacular casualty of traditional history.

INTRODUCTION

They have made up at least half the human race, but you could never tell that by looking at the books historians write." The new breed of historians is remedying that omission. They have written books about immigrant women and about working-class women who struggled for survival in cities and about black women who met the challenges of life in rural areas. They are telling the stories of women who, despite the barriers of tradition and economics, became lawyers and doctors and public figures.

The women's studies movement has also led scholars to question traditional interpretations of their respective disciplines. For example, the study of war has traditionally been an exercise in military and political analysis, an examination of strategies planned and executed by men. But scholars of women's history have pointed out that wars have also been periods of tremendous change and even opportunity for women, because the very absence of men on the home front enabled them to expand their educational, economic, and professional activities and to assume leadership in their homes.

The early scholars of women's history showed a unique brand of courage in choosing to investigate new subjects and take new approaches to old ones. Often, like their subjects, they endured criticism and even ostracism by their academic colleagues. But their efforts have unquestionably been worthwhile, because with the publication of each new study and book another piece of the historical patchwork is sewn into place, revealing an increasingly comprehensive picture of the role of women in our rich and varied history.

Such books on groups of women are essential, but books that focus on the lives of individuals are equally indispensable. Biographies can be inspirational, offering their readers the example of people with vision who have looked outside themselves for their goals and have often struggled against great obstacles to achieve them. Marian Anderson, for instance, had to overcome racial bigotry in order to perfect her art and perform as a concert singer. Isadora Duncan defied the rules of classical dance to find true artistic freedom. Jane Addams had to break down society's notions of the proper role for women in order to create new social institutions, notably the settlement house. All of these women had to come to terms both with themselves and with the world in which they lived. Only then could they move ahead as pioneers in their chosen callings.

Biography can inspire not only by adulation but also by realism. It helps us to see not only the qualities in others that we hope to emulate but also, perhaps, the weaknesses that made them "human." By helping us identify with the subject on a more personal level they help us to feel that we, too, can achieve such goals. We read about Eleanor Roosevelt, for example, who occupied a unique and seemingly enviable position as the wife of the president. Yet we can sympathize with her inner dilemma: an inherently shy woman who had to force herself to live a most public life in order to use her position to benefit others. We may not be able to imagine ourselves having the immense poetic talent of Emily Dickinson, but from her story we can understand the challenges faced by a creative woman who was expected to fulfill many family responsibilities. And though few of us will ever reach the level of athletic accomplishment displayed by Wilma Rudolph or Babe Zaharias, we can still appreciate their spirit, their overwhelming will to excel.

A biography is a multifaceted lens. It is first of all a magnification, the intimate examination of one particular life. But at the same time, it is a wide-angle lens, informing us about the world in which the subject lived. We come away from reading about one life knowing more about the social, political, and economic fabric of the time. It is for this reason, perhaps, that the great New England essayist Ralph Waldo Emerson wrote, in 1841, "There is properly no history: only biography." And it is also why biography, and particularly women's biography, will continue to fascinate writers and readers alike.

Betty Friedan

One of the leading figures in the women's rights movement, Betty Friedan founded the single largest group of feminists in America, the National Organization for Women (NOW), in 1966. Four years later, at NOW's annual convention, she unveiled her plans for the March for Equality, a nationwide demonstration in support of women's rights.

ONE

The March for Equality

At 5:30 P.M. on August 26, 1970, Betty Friedan clasped arms with the women standing next to her and started to march down New York City's Fifth Avenue. Behind them, a massive crowd of some 20,000 women fell into step. The March for Equality, an unprecedented show of strength by the city's feminists, had begun.

Friedan—author of *The Feminine Mystique*, the book that revitalized the women's movement in America shortly after it was published in 1963— had called on women all across the country to demonstrate for their rights on this summer day, exactly 50 years after an earlier generation of feminists had staged a massive demonstration to celebrate the passage of the Nineteenth Amendment, which gave women the right to vote. Feminists throughout America responded to Friedan's rallying cry: In Los Angeles, Chicago, Washington, D.C., Boston, and other cities, thousands of women took to the streets to rally, march, and show their support for the cause.

Friedan herself had organized the March for Equality in New York. Anticipating the event's importance, she had spoken to the press as if she were a general: "This is our hour of history. We're going to take it."

She seemed an unlikely leader for a revolution. A 49-year-old divorced mother of 3 children, Friedan had occasionally irritated both sympathizers and opponents with her brusque, aggressive manner. But even Friedan's detractors admitted that her eloquence, intelligence, and commitment to the women's movement made her an effective leader.

"She was the biggest thing that could have happened in feminism," said Flo Kennedy, a feminist activist and lawyer who joined Friedan on the March for Equality. "*The Feminine Mystique* was analysis that was so poignant and so well written. . . . Nothing before or since is comparable in terms of the impact on women's lives."

In *The Feminine Mystique*, Friedan examined women's status in American society and challenged other women— as she had challenged herself—to think of themselves as individuals, not only as someone's wife or mother. The critically acclaimed book reached more than 3 million readers and is generally credited with reintroducing the issue of women's liberation to the American public.

The core of Friedan's argument was that women must fully develop as human individuals. To do so, she urged them to go back to school and to work. "Equality and human dignity are not possible for women if they are not able to earn," she wrote in *The Feminine Mystique*. "Only economic independence can free a woman to marry for love, not for status or financial support, or to leave a loveless, intolerable, humiliating marriage, or to eat, dress, rest, and move if she plans not to marry."

In the years that immediately followed the publication of *The Feminine Mystique*, the participants in the women's movement came to hold widely divergent opinions on numerous specific issues. Yet when Friedan, the most visible feminist in the United States, announced the March for Equality, all factions agreed to participate. Controversial groups, which included the Redstockings, WITCH, and radical lesbians, united with more conventional organizations such as the National Coalition of American Nuns, the Young Women's Christian Association (YWCA), and, of course, the National Organization for Women (NOW), the single largest group of feminists in America. Friedan had founded NOW in 1966 and had served as its first president.

Over the course of several months in 1970, she had used the group's powerful lobbying network to organize the march. It was also through NOW that she had met many of the prominent women who marched and spoke on August 26. They included Shirley Chisholm, the black congresswoman from Brooklyn; Bella Abzug, an outspoken politician from the Bronx; Gloria Steinem, a journalist who later became a founder and editor of *Ms.* magazine; Kate Millet, author of *Sexual Politics*, a book that analyzed the portrayal of women by male writers; Joan Rivers, a well-known comedian; Gloria Vanderbilt, a wealthy heiress and successful businesswoman; and many others.

Powerful politicians who had not previously associated themselves with feminism also supported the March for Equality. Governor Nelson Rockefeller of New York recognized the movement by declaring August 26 Women's

Rights Day. Even the president of the United States, Richard Nixon, expressed a modicum of approval. "Let us all recognize," he said in an official proclamation, "that women surely have a still wider role to play in the political, economic and social life of our country."

The size and visibility of the march forced many men and women who had scoffed at participants in the women's movement and dismissed their fight for equality as a passing fad to recognize that the movement's members were serious, determined, and powerful.

The women's movement was not new. Abigail Adams, the nation's second First Lady, was also its first feminist; in 1776, she told her husband, John, "If particular care and attention is not paid to the Ladies, we are determined to foment a Rebellion." Susan B. Anthony and Elizabeth Cady Stanton were among the more notable feminists who carried on the struggle for women's rights during the 19th century. But since the approval of the Nineteenth Amendment, which enfranchised women, in 1920, the nation's women had not gained any other sig-

NOW members convene in New York City to make their final preparations for the March for Equality, which was held on August 26, 1970.

nificant rights. They still faced discrimination in almost every aspect of their life. Their education and employment opportunities were limited, often by law; in many states, a wife's income and property were completely under her husband's control; restaurants and bars that allowed only men to enter were commonplace. Even educators and psychologists who considered themselves progressive urged young women to dismiss the idea of pursuing careers and to devote themselves exclusively to their husbands and children. Women were, in effect, second-class citizens.

Support for the movement and its goals was not unanimous, and Friedan worried that critics might discourage potential marchers. On the morning of the March for Equality, the front page of the *New York Times* quoted conservative women's groups that claimed feminists were "ridiculous exhibitionists," "a band of wild lesbians," and "Communists." In the *New York Post*, columnist Harriet Van Horne had called them "uncombed, untidy, castrating shrews."

Mindful of her image in the media, Friedan had started the day by getting her gray hair curled at the Vidal Sassoon salon—a detail that the *Times* deemed newsworthy enough to report on the next day's front page. "We should try to be as pretty as we can," she told the reporter who followed her to the hairdresser. "It's good politics." On the day of the march, Friedan wore a fuchsia-colored dress adorned with a button depicting a clenched red fist in the center of a white circle atop a cross, a longtime medical symbol for women. "Today all women are beautiful," she told a reporter.

Although Friedan could count on the members of NOW and the other feminist groups to meet her at the corner of 59th Street and Fifth Avenue, it was important that word of the march spread throughout the city: Friedan wanted as many American women as possible to join her and her sister activists in their march and call for equality. Nevertheless, doubts about the turnout gnawed at her self-confidence throughout the day. She worried up to the last minute that only a few activists might attend, and she would be publicly humiliated. More important, the women's movement might be crippled.

Organizers staged small demonstrations around the city before the march's 5:30 starting time to spark the interest of the public and the media. When Friedan arrived at City Hall to speak at a noon ceremony along with Steinem, Abzug, and New York City consumer affairs commissioner Bess Meyerson, she was dismayed that only a few hundred people, mostly men, showed up. Still, the press was there, and the deputy mayor officially acknowledged the day as Women's Equality Day in New York. Friedan and the other speakers outlined their demands: equal pay for equal work, a chance at jobs then reserved for men, reform of laws restricting abortion, and community-supported child care.

Friedan spent the rest of the afternoon trooping around the city, lending

The March for Equality in full stride: In a show of strength, thousands of women parade along Fifth Avenue in New York City. Even though some of the marchers voiced their individual concerns, all of them were united in the drive to generate interest in the issue of full equality for women.

her support to small demonstrations. She joined NOW women to protest at the New York Stock Exchange because it employed only a handful of women. She "liberated" a males-only dining room in a restaurant on Fulton Street. At an East Side supermarket, she demonstrated against products that were advertised with images that degraded women. But the main event was to be the march down Fifth Avenue.

At around 5:00 P.M., as most New Yorkers were ending their workday, Friedan stepped off a bus on Manhattan's East Side, aware that the most important part of the day's activities was just beginning. Her lingering fears vanished when she saw thousands of women and men assembled for the march, waiting for her. The turnout, she told a *Time* magazine reporter, "exceeded my wildest dreams." Smiling,

17

Feminist Bella Abzug was among the speakers at the rally in New York City's Bryant Park that concluded the March for Equality. She was later elected to the New York State Senate with the backing of the National Women's Political Caucus, a lobbyist group cofounded by Friedan.

she greeted her friends and supporters, moved to the front of the crowd, and led them forward.

"I remember looking back, jumping up to see over marchers' heads," Friedan wrote later. "I never saw so many women; they stretched back for so many blocks you couldn't see the end. . . . We overflowed till we filled the whole of Fifth Avenue. . . . It was the first great nationwide action of women."

The marchers headed downtown, filling the avenue from sidewalk to sidewalk. The police, who had not expected such numbers, were forced to divert traffic. Some marchers carried banners that read Women of the World United. Others held aloft signs such as Sisterhood Is Powerful and *Liberté, égalité, sororité* (Liberty, equality, sisterhood). Some carried babies on their back; some raised their fists, chanted, and cheered. Women with gray hair and teenagers in bell-bottom trousers strode along, side by side. Among them marched a sprinkling of men.

As the demonstrators proceeded past crowds of women gathered on the sidewalks, Friedan and other marchers continually called out, "Come join us, sisters." Many did, swelling the ranks of the marchers.

When the demonstrators reached the end of their march at Bryant Park on 42nd Street, behind the main branch of the New York Public Library, they rallied there, listening and cheering to impassioned speeches by feminist activists, writers, and politicians. Gloria Steinem, sporting her trademark long hair and aviator glasses, introduced speakers at the rally. As night fell, Kate Millet told the crowd, "Today is the beginning of a new movement. Today is the end of millenniums of oppression." Other speakers included Bella Abzug and feminist activist Ti-Grace Atkinson.

Friedan told the rally, "In the religion of my ancestors, there was a prayer that Jewish men said every morning. They prayed, 'Thank thee, Lord, that I was not born a woman.' Today . . . all women are going to be able to say . . . 'Thank thee, Lord, that I was born a woman.'" Cheers and applause thundered through the crowd when she continued, "After tonight, the politics of this nation will never be the same again. . . . There is no way any man, woman or child can escape the nature of our revolution."

In an editorial the next day, the *New York Times* offered qualified support for the movement. "Now all that remains is for laws and popular attitude to catch up with the new facts of equality," it said. Yet achieving "all that remains" took years of tenacious lobbying and effort.

The *Times* also severely underestimated the long-term effects of Friedan's efforts when it stated, "There could well be thousands of additional women in engineering, architecture, medicine and other traditionally masculine professions." In fact, in the years that followed, changes in attitude and in the law resulted in *millions* of women entering those fields—and a revolution in the American way of life.

Friedan during her youth. She grew up in Peoria, Illinois, where she excelled at school and also enjoyed writing and acting.

TWO

"The Passion of the Mind"

Betty Friedan was born Elizabeth Naomi Goldstein on February 4, 1921, in Peoria, Illinois. Betty, her older sister, Amy, and younger brother, Harry, grew up in their parents' large, red-brick house, which featured a big front porch and a view of Bradley Park, in the upper-middle-class area of Peoria called the Bluff. Their father, Harry Goldstein, owned a jewelry store, and their mother, Miriam, was active in community affairs.

Harry was a kindly man who read extensively. Although he was an immigrant from Europe who never learned to speak English perfectly, he became a prominent, successful businessman. He began by selling collar buttons from a street-corner stand; before long, he had his own store, Goldstein's, which became known locally as "the Tiffany's of Peoria."

Despite his success, Harry and his trim, elegant wife, who was the daughter of a doctor, often fought about money. As a young woman, Miriam held high ambitions that were soon frustrated. She had wanted to go to prestigious Smith College in Massachusetts, but her parents insisted she attend a local college instead. Afterwards, she worked as a society reporter for a Peoria newspaper, but she gave up her job to marry and have children—as women were expected to do in the early decades of the 20th century.

A striking, vivacious, and athletic woman who loved to entertain, Miriam, who was 17 years younger than her husband, demanded that he provide a fairly grand way of life for their family. They hired live-in servants, and Miriam's taste in clothes and household decor proved quite expensive.

When the Great Depression of the 1930s reduced Harry's business, Miriam pressured him relentlessly to earn more money.

Peace at the Goldstein household was disturbed for other reasons as well. Tension between Miriam and her oldest daughter was high. To Miriam's dismay, Betty had to wear metal braces on her legs until she was three to correct their tendency to bow. Although early photographs of Betty show her to have been an attractive girl with large brown deep-lidded eyes, her mother felt that Betty's prominent nose, which she had inherited from her father, made her unattractive. Later, Betty wore orthodontic braces and eyeglasses, reinforcing Miriam's belief that Betty was the smart but plain daughter and Amy, a year and a half younger, was the pretty one—thereby instilling a bitter rivalry between the sisters.

Betty recalled that her mother "was very critical of me and made me feel very insecure." Miriam, who took meticulous care of her appearance and was considered one of the best-dressed women in Peoria, nagged Betty to follow her example. Loud arguments erupted because Betty insisted on dressing sloppily and keeping her room untidy. She vastly preferred reading to primping and housekeeping.

As the children grew older, Harry showed his pride in his oldest daughter by often boasting about her scholastic achievements to his customers. Around the dinner table, he would ask his children questions about current events. "The serious questions about

Miriam Goldstein, Betty's mother, was prominent in community affairs and edited the society page in the local Peoria newspaper before she gave these activities up to raise her three children.

what was going on in the world would always be directed at Betty and the frivolous ones at me," Amy remembered many years later. "And in that way we began to build our sense of who we were."

Betty was such a bookworm that her father limited the number of library books she could take out each week to five, a restriction she thought cruel.

Her parents were so concerned about her overwhelming preference for books over dolls and her tendency to be temperamental that they took her to a child psychologist. He told them to leave the brilliant girl to her own devices.

Betty later revealed her thoughts about her childhood and adolescence, in a 23-page autobiographical essay she wrote for school at the age of 17. She described the three years before she entered high school as "years of almost perfect happiness." Before the advent of television, children, by necessity, relied on their ingenuity to invent games—and when it came to inventiveness and imagination, Betty was unrivaled. In her essay, she wrote about friends with whom she played "dressups," a game that involved taking their mothers' old evening dresses and scarves up to Betty's attic. "We took turns choosing until the whole collection was divided and then we became other people, princesses, beautiful, sophisticated heiresses, movie stars, spies." Then they created a game called Mystery, in which they imagined each of their houses as "a potential den of thieves. We tapped all the walls for secret passages and wrote notes in secret codes." Later, they turned to playing detective. "We had secret signals and religiously kept a clue book. There was a little house situated near the boundary of the park across from [a nearby] house which we knew was a smuggler's hideout."

As Betty Goldstein's group of friends grew older, they formed a club and played Post Office and kissing games.

Harry Goldstein, Betty's father, was a successful businessman who turned his jewelry store, Goldstein's, into the "Tiffany's of Peoria."

"We thought we were very wicked and daring," Betty recalled. They went roller skating and attended basketball games and dances. Betty began writing skits and acting in school plays. In the summer, she went to picnics at the country club and enjoyed horseback riding and canoeing at sleep-away camps; in 1933, the family attended the World's Fair, held in nearby Chicago. Throughout these years, Betty continued to read voraciously.

When Betty entered Central High School in 1934, she was full of optimistic expectations. But they were crushed when most of her friends were invited, or "rushed," into high school sororities, and she was excluded. Betty was convinced she was discriminated against because she was Jewish.

Shortly thereafter, Betty's crowd of friends broke up. As a result, she often felt lonely. "That year I think I began to have an inferiority complex," she wrote in her teenage autobiography. Her brother and sister agree that some of the ostracism she endured was due to anti-Semitism, but the awkwardness of adolescence was also responsible. "I thought myself a social outcast and I plumbed the depths of misery," Betty wrote with great dramatic flair. "At night I looked out at the park from my window and thought of the others all having a good time and I felt *so* sorry for myself. Every time anyone spoke to me my feelings got hurt. . . . Life held nothing in store. I decided that I would probably never get married because I didn't have any sex appeal."

Although Betty may have bewailed her lack of sex appeal, even at a young age she displayed her surprisingly strong-minded views about marriage in another part of the essay. "I know this," Betty wrote. "I don't want to marry a man and keep house for him and be the mother of his children and nothing else. I want to do something with my life—to have an absorbing interest. I want success and fame."

The essay also provides glimpses of two different sides of Betty's character.

When events went her way, she was in her element, and her gregarious nature came to the fore. "I was a leader—or 'bossy'—organizing clubs etc. from the fourth grade on," she said. Her ability to rally people and inspire them to activity (which later helped her galvanize the women's movement) became apparent early. But the bitterness and insecurity she felt when her childhood friends no longer stayed in the tightly knit group she preferred was also part of her character; years later, when her colleagues at NOW and other feminists moved in directions of which she did not approve, Betty reacted as she had in high school—with a flare of temper and personal sense of injury.

However, even during those difficult freshman and sophomore years, when her old friends, as she described it, "didn't want me around," Betty did have some girlfriends with whom she walked to school and listened to music. She also joined a theater group at school, which she called "a grand experience." And always, she had her schoolwork. "Schoolwork was my only escape," she maintained. "I was good at it and I loved it."

One afternoon when Betty came home from school feeling particularly lonely and sad, she made a vow to herself: "If they don't like me, at least they're going to respect me." She developed a strategy based on her observation that "there were two ways to be a success in high school—either to be very popular, or to be very prominent and successful in activities." She chose the latter course.

Starting in her junior year, Betty's social life improved. She began writing a column that she called Cabbages and Kings for the school newspaper; she acted in several school plays and directed a one-act play; she entered a speech contest and won second prize (although her disappointment at not winning the top prize was so acute that she considered the contest a low point). She went on a few dates and made new friends. "I made up my mind that never again would I let myself be hurt by depending too much on one or two close friends. I decided to have many good friends." Soon, her house became an after-school gathering place. "My whole personality changed," Betty recalled. "I stopped being so miserably self-conscious."

During the summer before her senior year, Betty learned to drive and taught herself to touch-type. Then, in her last year at Central High, she fulfilled a dream by winning the school's best actress award for her performance as the madwoman in *Jane Eyre* and helped start a literary magazine, *Tide*. Toward the end of the year, she gushed, "It is fun having lots of friends and having

Friedan (front row, center) with fellow members of her high school literary society. At school, she participated in a number of clubs devoted to drama and writing.

QUILL AND SCROLL

Friedan (center) performs in a play at Smith College, where she continued to take part in extracurricular activities while maintaining an excellent academic record.

more to do than you can possibly do and being so rushed and busy that you cannot stop to take a breath." She ended the year in triumph by being named valedictorian of her class.

In the fall of 1939, Betty Goldstein left for Smith, the women's college in Northampton, Massachusetts, that her mother had wanted to attend. Although Betty despaired during her freshman year over her lack of boyfriends, her last three years at Smith were among the happiest of her life. She recalled, "After Peoria, Smith, for me, was . . . the passion of the mind."

Studying, reading, getting involved with liberal causes to help the poor and underprivileged—Goldstein did everything with furious energy. During her sophomore year, she had to be hospitalized because of a collapsed lung; nevertheless, she finished the year with an A in every class. She became editor in chief of the college newspaper and

In 1942, Friedan graduated summa cum laude from Smith College and was the valedictorian of her class. "I was that girl with all A's," she said later, "and I wanted boys worse than anything."

managing editor of the literary magazine. She even took a class in medieval literature, although the subject did not especially interest her; rather, she was intrigued by the challenge of studying with the most difficult professor on campus. One day, he yelled at her, "Miss Goldstein, you lack humility! You are too arrogant, you lack humility!"

Most summers during college, Goldstein worked in jobs related to her major, psychology. She worked one summer with the eminent behavioral psychologist Kurt Lewin at the University of Iowa, assisting in early experiments in group dynamics. During another summer, she took a job as an intern at a mental hospital in the suburbs of New York City.

When workers for the college began organizing into a union, Goldstein wrote articles in their support. Union activity was considered controversial by many Americans, and the suspicion that unions were somehow socialist, communist, or un-American was widespread. Starting in the 1930s, the Federal Bureau of Investigation (FBI) began surveillance of American citizens who it suspected were subversives, and Goldstein's activities on behalf of the workers attracted the bureau's attention. The FBI compiled a report on her that read in part, "Subject [Goldstein] considered radical and leftist . . . subject was forever-lastingly opposing college politics and policies." The report added, "The subject was one of the outstanding students to graduate from

After graduating from Smith College, Friedan won a prestigious fellowship to study at the University of California at Berkeley with Erik Erikson, a renowned psychologist and researcher. While at Berkeley, she was awarded a fellowship for further postgraduate study but turned it down.

this college in recent years. She won the scholarship prize as a Freshman; she was elected to Sigma Chi Sorority; was a Sophia Smith Scholar in 1939–40; was elected to Phi Beta Kappa in her senior year and won the Alumni Fellowship."

When Goldstein graduated summa cum laude and the valedictorian of her class, a college administrator told her family, "Betty has the most outstanding record of any student ever matriculated at Smith. Her thesis is an original contribution to the field of behavioral science. It could stand for a Ph.D." Despite all her achievements, Betty said later, "I was that girl with all A's and I wanted boys worse than anything . . . with all the brilliance, I saw myself becoming the old maid college teacher."

Goldstein won a research fellowship at the University of California at Berkeley, and she went there for a year to study with the well-known psychoanalyst Erik Erikson. It was another happy year; she even met a young man and fell in love. Then she won another, more lucrative fellowship. If she were to accept the stipend, it would mean committing herself to work for a Ph.D. and a career as a professional psychologist. She talked the matter over with her boyfriend. "We walked in the Berke-ley hills," she recalled, "and he said, 'Nothing can come of this, between us. I'll never win a fellowship like yours.' " Goldstein turned down the offer, fearful of intimidating him. "It was the kind of either-or situation that is my constant burden in life," she said later. "Either I pursue my career or I subli-mate my wishes to a man's."

In any event, her frustration may have induced the asthma attacks that suddenly afflicted her. That same year, 1943, her father died. Betty and her siblings believed that he had worked himself to death.

Miriam Goldstein proceeded to run the jewelry shop for another 10 years. Betty, who did not visit home very often during her college years, rarely visited Peoria after her father's death. "I became very estranged from my mother," she recalled, "very critical of her. Part of it was normal growing up, becoming aware of one's own self. But I had to do it more than most."

Friedan with her husband, Carl, and eldest son, Daniel. During the early years of her marriage, she penned articles that glorified married life. Yet she was anything but a truly conventional housewife.

THREE

"The Happy Housewife Heroine"

Still tormented by her asthma, Betty Goldstein ended the relationship with her boyfriend in 1943 and moved to New York City, where she shared an apartment on Waverly Place in Greenwich Village with some friends from Smith and Vassar. She took an editorial job with a labor newspaper, the *Federated Press*, and immersed herself in political activity and the intellectual life of the city. She participated in Marxist discussion groups, and one day gave a street-corner speech in support of Henry Wallace (the U.S. vice-president from 1941 to 1945, who ran for president in 1948 on the Progressive party ticket, campaigning for closer U.S. relations with the Soviet Union).

At her *Federated Press* job, Goldstein wrote dozens of articles on labor-related subjects—articles about unions

trying to organize, companies that exploited workers, and workers dealing with on-the-job conditions during World War II. At the earliest stage of her writing career, she demonstrated her interest in women's issues. In an article entitled "Pretty Posters Won't Stop Turnover of Women in Industry," she quoted a female union official who told her, "Women still have two jobs to do. Until the government solves the problem of food rationing, prices, child care—so that women won't have to worry about their children on the job, or take time off to stand for hours in line to buy dinner or to do their laundry—there's going to be absenteeism and turnover in industry."

In the early 1940s, when millions of American men were away from their regular jobs because of the war, the ensuing labor shortage convinced industry and the government to hire women—although only for the duration of the war. Many women went to work in the munitions factories, and for the first time black women—whose job opportunities had previously been limited to domestic work—were able to overcome the racial discrimination against them and find work in more prestigious and higher-paying fields such as nursing and clerical work. In general, throughout the war American women gained the opportunity to do the kind of skilled and managerial work that had been previously reserved for men.

Because it was important to the war effort and the national economy that women go to work in industry, the federal government promoted this trend by creating a poster and propaganda campaign featuring pictures of strong, happy women in the factory. Magazine covers and advertising promoted the same images. Soon, the character of Rosie the Riveter, a factory worker who was written up in a widely published magazine article, became a prominent role model.

After World War II, intellectuals such as Goldstein expressed their concern over many issues: civil rights for blacks; relations with Russia, China, and the United Nations; and the abuse of power by the House Un-American Activities Committee (HUAC), a government committee that accused, interrogated, and publicly humiliated Americans who were suspected of being Communists. One thing intellec-tuals did not seem to worry about, however, was the status of women, which had changed abruptly following World War II.

When the war ended in September 1945, the massive influx of returning servicemen had an unprecedented effect on American society. Sixteen million American soldiers had participated in the war, and after years of fighting and hardships they eagerly sought the comforts of home.

Friedan wrote later, "When the men came back there was a headlong rush into marriage. The lonely years when husbands or husbands-to-be were away at war ... made women particularly vulnerable to the feminine mystique." During this time, many young women who formerly would have attended and graduated from college left school or did not enroll—instead, they got married. In America, the average age of a woman when she married dropped from 23 to 20, and for a man it fell from 25 to 23. An astounding jump in the birth rate—the so-called "baby boom" —soon followed, and by the end of the 1950s the annual rate of population increase in the United States had outstripped that of all other Western nations, as well as the rate in such less-developed countries as India and Pakistan.

The return of servicemen not only fueled economic forces but also reaffirmed cultural expectations that women be unemployed and remain in the home. Women who had taken jobs in industry while men were at war gave up their positions to the returning vet-

Throughout World War II, women—including those who cleaned spark plugs for military vehicles—filled jobs formerly held by men. Despite their contributions to the war effort, women did not enjoy a rise in economic status after the war.

erans. This change in the structure of American society was reflected most noticeably by magazines filled with articles about how women could best help their men by being devoted wives and homemakers. Even if women wanted to continue working—even if they had no husband coming back to support them—companies often forced them out to make jobs available for the former soldiers. The prevailing view was: Men were breadwinners, women were housewives. Although a young woman might not particularly wish to wed, the structure of American society often propelled her into marriage.

When companies advertised products for the home, they always showed women wearing aprons, doing the laundry, waxing floors, cooking, or doing dishes. "The happy housewife heroine," as Friedan dubbed the image in *The Feminine Mystique*, became a sort of national icon—and an important consumer much courted by advertisers. These images of women were so pervasive that it became difficult for many people to remember that women could have an identity outside the home. During the late 1940s and throughout the 1950s, women were very rarely portrayed as careerists in literary fiction and film. Friedan remembered that 1949 "saw the last of the spirited, brave, adventurous heroines who had filled the magazines and movies in the thirties and forties—the Claudette Colbert, Myrna Loy, Bette Davis, Rosalind Russell, and Katharine Hepburn types. These heroines, in the end, got their man, but they were usually working toward some goal or vision of their own, independent and determined and passionately involved with the world. They were . . . less kittenish than the Doris Day little housewife that followed."

As Goldstein entered her mid-twenties, the entire thrust of American culture focused on family life. Like young women throughout America, she was not immune to societal pressures.

Soon after she moved to a basement apartment on West 86th Street, a friend introduced her to Carl Friedan, a handsome young man from Boston. During the war, he had managed the Soldier Show Company in Europe, and afterward he managed summer stock theater. He was charming and amusing, a boyfriend who "made me feel not alone," she said. They married in a brief civil ceremony at City Hall in June 1947, followed by a small Jewish ceremony performed by a rabbi.

Betty Friedan continued working while she was pregnant with her first child, Daniel, who was born in 1948, and after a year's maternity leave she went back to work, a move that was considered slightly unusual for a woman with a young child. During the early years of their marriage, however, the Friedans were fairly conventional. They moved to a 4½-room garden apartment in nearby Queens, where Betty threw herself into the life of a mother and homemaker.

When Friedan let it be known that she was pregnant with her second child, Jonathan, who was born in 1952,

Housework and child rearing dominated the life of most women in the 1950s. Manufacturers and advertisers encouraged them to aspire to the role of the "happy housewife heroine," which was idealized in glossy images that filled magazines and television screens throughout the decade.

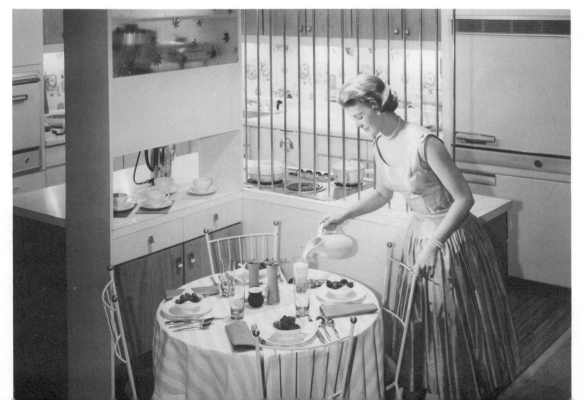

While working as a writer for The Federated Press, *a New York City labor newspaper, Friedan (far right) was introduced to her future husband, Carl (second from left), by mutual friends. They were married in June 1947.*

she was fired from her job. Fortunately, Carl found a more lucrative job in advertising, and the family soon had enough money to move to suburban Rockland County, settling into an 11-room Victorian house in the village of Grandview. The residence boasted a view across the Hudson River, a long front porch, and woods in the back. The house became a bit more crowded in 1956, when a daughter, Emily, was born.

In many ways, the Friedans were living the American dream. Yet Betty Friedan was never a truly conventional housewife. One neighbor called her a "typical career woman you wouldn't ask to borrow a cup of sugar." Neighbors expelled Emily from a school car pool because when it was her mother's turn to drive, Friedan sent a taxi to pick up the children.

During this period, Friedan wrote free-lance articles for women's magazines, which tended to promote what Friedan later labeled "the feminine mystique." The editors assigned writers to produce articles about bringing up children, cooking, decorating, sewing, and household advice. Years later, a woman editor explained to Friedan why the magazines commissioned only these sorts of articles. Female editors, she said, "began to feel embarrassed about being career women ourselves. There was this terrible fear that we were losing our femininity. We kept looking for ways to help women accept their feminine role."

The free-lance articles that Friedan penned conformed to popular formulas.

She wrote articles for *Redbook* and *Ladies' Home Journal* with such titles as "Millionaire's Wife" and "Two Are an Island." In "I Was Afraid to Have a Baby," Friedan wrote about the actress Julie Harris, who claimed, "Suddenly it didn't seem so important to be a great actress, to drive myself for my career. I'd almost rather not have one, I thought, sitting there. Just stay home and have babies and not have so many things cluttering up my life." This article, which was quite typical of Friedan's work, served two functions. As a profile of a famous actress, it gave housewives a glimpse of the glamorous Hollywood life. At the same time, it reinforced the idea that it was good to be a housewife, for Harris denigrates her career. Later, Friedan expressed embarrassment about having written these articles.

Young women were actually more career-minded during the 1920s and 1930s than they were in the 1950s. In 1930, women made up nearly 50 percent of Americans employed in professions; 30 years later, women made up only 35 percent of the nation's professional work force. And in 1920, 47 percent of all college students were women; in 1958, only 35 percent were.

One of the reasons that women in the 1920s were more independent was their victory in gaining passage of the Nineteenth Amendment, which gave American women the right to vote. Having won the vote after a long, hard battle, women appreciated their freedom and their potential power. No issue comparable to the drive for suffrage

Betty and Carl Friedan at home, supervising a birthday party for one of their children.

united women in the 1930s, however. As women ceased to fight actively for their freedom, they began to lose some of the gains they had made.

By the 1950s, despite technological improvements that made it easier to keep a home organized—and theoretically, at least, freed women to work outside the home—the percentage of women who were working was the lowest it had been since 1910. There had not been so few female college professors since 1879. Of all doctorates granted in the United States, fewer than 1 out of every 10 were awarded to women in 1956; in 1920 the proportion had been 1 out of 6.

American women fared badly not only in comparison with earlier generations but also when compared with women in other Western nations. In Sweden, Britain, and France, the proportion of women with education above the high school level increased from the 1930s to the 1950s; but in the United States, it decreased. In France, women participated in the medical profession, as did women in America; but the proportion of Frenchwomen in medicine was five times larger than the proportion of American women in the profession. In terms of the decline of their rights, status, and identity in society, the 1950s were the worst decade for women in the history of America.

One day around 1956, Friedan overheard a rare working woman—a scientist—talking about her career in physics. Fascinated, Friedan interviewed the person and wrote an article for *Harper's* magazine. Friedan's editor, George Brockaway, liked it so much he proposed she expand it to a book-length manuscript that he could publish. Friedan thought the offer over carefully before refusing. Being asked to write a book boosted her confidence. But she decided that if she was going to write a book, it would be on a subject of her own expertise and her own choosing.

Friedan and her daughter, Emily, pose for a snapshot in their family room. For five years, Betty juggled her time between running the household and writing and researching her first book, The Feminine Mystique.

FOUR

The Feminine Mystique

As Betty Friedan prepared in 1957 to attend her 15th college reunion, she did not regard her professional achievements over the past decade and a half with satisfaction. Being a housewife and a writer for popular women's magazines did not meet the expectations she had set for herself when she was 20 years old. After all, she had been the valedictorian of her class, and her professors and classmates had predicted a bright future for her.

For the reunion, Friedan was assigned to poll her classmates to find out what they had been doing since graduation. She composed a lengthy questionnaire and sent it to her fellow students, asking them questions about every aspect of their lives: What difficulties have you found in working out your role as a woman? What are the chief satisfactions and frustrations of your life today? Has your education at Smith College adequately prepared you for adulthood? Have you lived up to your own expectations?

Friedan assumed that her classmates were living the American dream. After all, they had entered college with many advantages. Because Smith is an expensive school, most of its students come from privileged homes. Moreover, it is very selective in its admission policies; the majority of its students come from the nation's best high schools.

The replies to the questionnaire shocked Friedan. The overwhelming majority of respondents were disappointed with their lives; they felt something was missing. Of the 200 alumnae that Friedan interviewed, 89 percent were housewives. Their answers revealed their bitterness at failing to use their education and talents. But rather than feeling that their education had been a waste of time, 80 percent of them said their main regret was that they had not seriously planned to apply their education to professional work.

A woman who was married to a doctor and had three children told Friedan, "The tragedy was, nobody ever looked us in the eye and said you have to decide what you want to do with your life, besides being your husband's wife and children's mother. . . . I always knew as a child that I was going to grow up and go to college and then get married, and that's as far as a girl has to think."

Friedan also discovered that each of these women thought that she alone felt this despair and discontent, when in fact a generation of women shared it. Most women blamed themselves or believed they were neurotic. Friedan called this affliction, common to so many women, "the problem that has no name."

After analyzing the questionnaires, Friedan came to the conclusion that for these women education was not the enemy; keeping house as a way of life was. She subsequently wrote an article on the subject and gave it the ironic title "The Togetherness Woman," then took it to *McCall's* magazine, whose editors had coined the term *Togetherness Woman* to describe their ideal reader. For the first time in Friedan's writing career, the editor rejected one of her articles because it was too different from the image of women that the magazine presented.

Friedan then tried *Ladies' Home Journal*, but the editor wanted to alter her argument to say that *education* was the obstacle to happy domestic life. Friedan quickly withdrew the article and submitted it to *Redbook*. The editor there asked her to expand it to encompass interviews with younger women. Friedan complied and found that women who graduated from college during the 15 years between 1942 and 1957 suffered in even greater numbers from the problem that has no name.

When Friedan brought her expanded article back to *Redbook*, the editor rejected it. Friedan's message was angrier than he had expected and conflicted with the editorial policy of the magazine. Disappointed, she gave up on her article for a few weeks.

Friedan's enthusiasm was renewed after she attended a lecture by author Vance Packard, whose bestselling book *The Hidden Persuaders* warned about the insidious effects of television advertising on viewers. He had originally intended to write an article on the subject but decided to write a book instead after every magazine to which he offered his piece turned it down. Encouraged by Packard's story, Friedan decided that her insights and research into the problem that has no name warranted a book. She contacted George Brockaway, then an editor at W. W. Norton and Company, and he offered her a $1,000 advance. When

"Mostly I find writing so painful I wonder what makes me do it," Friedan once told a reporter. Nevertheless, she chose to expand "The Togetherness Woman," an article that several magazines had rejected, into the much lengthier work, The Feminine Mystique.

Friedan signed the contract, she told Brockaway that she could deliver a completed manuscript in a year.

During the early stages of the project, Friedan spent three days a week researching her subject in the New York Public Library. She then wrote out her findings on legal pads in the dining room of her home. Her research revealed dispiriting statistics about the decline of the status of women in the first 50 years of the 20th century. "Not long ago, women dreamed and fought for equality, their own place in the world," she wrote. "What happened to their dreams; when did women decide to give up the world and go back home?"

Like Vance Packard, Friedan learned that advertising affected more than which products American consumers decided to buy—it sometimes changed their attitude toward their way of life. She found that "companies which made a big profit selling us all those washing machines, dryers, freezers and second cars, were overselling us on the bliss of domesticity in order to sell us more things. Even the most radical of us, in our innocence, wanted those pressure cookers."

Friedan's conclusions ranged far beyond an examination of the effect of advertising on American life. So extensive did the book become that the research and writing took not one year but five years. "Neither my husband nor my publisher nor anyone else who knew about it thought that I would ever finish it," she said later. "Mostly I find writing so painful I wonder what makes me do it." Nevertheless, she persevered.

Friedan knew that her book would be attacked by both men and women who felt threatened by her ideas. Therefore, to support her premise that women were wasting their lives by staying at home and that as men's equals they deserved a place in the wider world, she tried to refute every argument that might possibly be put forward by opponents to women's equality.

Psychologists and psychiatrists who used Freudian theories in their work usually accepted Freud's characterization of women as "childlike dolls, who existed in terms only of man's love, to love man and serve his needs." Friedan devoted an entire chapter to a closely reasoned criticism of Freud's ideas—an attack for which her background in psychology well equipped her. In the 1950s and early 1960s, women who sought assistance from a Freudian psychologist for the problem that has no name were usually counseled to accept their femininity, the core of which was women's natural passivity. A well-adjusted woman welcomed her femininity and followed her husband's lead; an ill-adjusted one struggled to develop her mind and personality and find a place in the world outside the home.

"What is femininity," Friedan wrote, "if it can be destroyed by an education which makes the mind grow, or induced by not letting the mind grow?" In the late 1950s, when Friedan was writing her book, questioning the pop-

Margaret Mead, an influential anthropologist, irked Friedan by endorsing the accepted views about femininity in her writings while ignoring them in her own life. Friedan devoted a chapter in The Feminine Mystique *to an analysis of Mead's work.*

ular notion of femininity was a revolutionary act.

Another chapter challenged the widely read opinions of Margaret Mead, the renowned anthropologist and popular author. Mead, who studied primitive societies and applied lessons learned from them to modern life, gave mixed messages about women's status in her writings. Although she encouraged men to help with household chores, she also suggested that ambition in a woman was a neurotic characteristic, even though Mead herself was both a mother and a highly respected professional. Friedan suggested that women should emulate Mead's own way of life rather than heed Mead's writings on femininity, which Friedan regarded as hypocritical.

Friedan devoted another chapter to an analysis of and attack on educators who, she said, "segregated recent generations of able American women as surely as separate-but-equal education segregated able American Negroes from the opportunity to realize their full abilities in the mainstream of American life." Friedan was referring to the trend, even at prestigious women's colleges, to encourage students to become housewives and "follow their proper feminine role." Some professors felt it was their duty to steer students away from careers. Friedan was particularly incensed that Radcliffe College offered an "Institute for Executives' Wives," instead of an institute for female executives.

Furthermore, young women, Friedan

Friedan's interviews with female college students in the late 1950s led to a disturbing revelation: Many of them felt they had to conform to the prevailing notion of women as homemakers and childbearers and deny any interest they might have in pursuing another type of career.

said, were being taught not to "work too hard, think too often, ask too many questions." Her interviews with 1950s college students provided appalling evidence for her argument. One young

46

girl whom Friedan interviewed told her: "We don't want careers. Our parents expect us to go to college. Everybody goes. You're a social outcast at home if you don't. But a girl who got serious about anything she studied—like wanting to go on and do research—would be peculiar, unfeminine. I guess everybody wants to graduate with a diamond ring on her finger. That's the important thing."

Another young woman told Friedan: "I got so excited about my work I would sometimes go into the library at eight in the morning and not come out till ten at night. I even thought I might want to go on to graduate school or law school and really use my mind. Suddenly, I was afraid of what would happen. I wanted to lead a rich full life. I want to marry, have children, have a nice house . . . so this year I'm trying to lead a well rounded life. I take courses but I don't read eight books and still feel like reading a ninth . . . the other way was harder, and more exciting. I don't know why I stopped. Maybe I just lost courage."

The more Friedan talked to women, the more she felt she must exhort them to recognize the fallacies of the popular image of femininity and reject them. Her impassioned argument in *The Feminine Mystique* read in part:

> To do the work that you are capable of doing is the mark of maturity . . . it is the mystique of feminine fulfillment and the immaturity it breeds that prevents women from doing the work of which they are capable.

By the promise of magical fulfillment through marriage, the feminine mystique arrests their development at an infantile level, short of personal identity.

Self-actualizing people invariably have a commitment, a sense of mission in life that makes them live in a very large human world, a frame of reference beyond privatism and preoccupation with the petty details of life.

However long it may take for women's magazines, sociologists, educators, and psychoanalysts to correct the mistakes that perpetuate the feminine mystique, a woman must deal with them now, in the prejudices, mistaken fears, and unnecessary dilemmas voiced by her husband; her friends and neighbors; perhaps her minister, priest or rabbi.

Upon publication of the book in 1963, Friedan sent her mother a copy, along with a note: "With all the troubles we have had, you gave me the power to break through the feminine mystique which will not, I think, be a problem any longer for Emily. I hope you accept the book for what it is, an affirmation of the values of your life and mine."

The book received mixed reviews. *Life* magazine said the book was "as disruptive of cocktail party conversation and women's club discussions as a tear-gas bomb. Its author has been vilified and praised in about equal quantities." The *New York Times Book Review* was critical: "It is superficial to blame the 'culture' and its handmaidens, the women's magazines, as she does. . . . To paraphrase a famous line,

Friedan relaxes in an armchair at her home in Grandview, New York. Less tranquil times were soon to follow.

'The fault dear Mrs. Friedan is not in our culture, but in ourselves.' " The *Detroit News* review was reverential, however. "For sheer impact on the lives of American women, no book written in the sixties compares with Betty Friedan's *The Feminine Mystique*, sometimes called the *Uncle Tom's Cabin* of the women's liberation movement."

When *The Feminine Mystique* finally reached bookstores, five years after Friedan began writing it, she did not sit back and wait for her message to spread. Ready and eager to promote the book, she began lecturing to college audiences, women's groups, and professional organizations all over the country. She also went on every talk show that invited her. Although Friedan was brusque with hosts, her delivery was sharp and she was an effective speaker, sometimes even a funny one. Interviewers may have found her a difficult guest, but television audiences, who did not have to respond to her aggressive verbal challenges, often thought her refreshingly honest and dynamic. Slowly, sales of the book took off.

Letters from thousands of readers poured in. A woman in Iowa wrote, "Thank God someone had the courage to write it. It struck at the center of my being. I am finally confident of myself and my desire to launch the career I've wanted for so long. The last of the cobwebs of guilt have been swept away, and what a marvelous free feeling! The release of women from this subtle bondage can only be good and right. How can it help but add a new dimen-

sion to the lives of the male as well as the female. . . . I have been able now to rid myself of the resentment I have felt toward my husband in particular and men in general. I am on the threshold of a new life. I feel excited for the first time in years."

Other readers sent Friedan angry letters: "I happen to love the rewards of being completely passive, with just the hint of the aggressor at the right time. I don't want to compete with my husband. I want to respect and admire and love him. My whole life isn't *completely* centered around my home and family, but you can bet your bottom dollar 95 percent of it is, and I love it. I'm sick of having my station referred to as trapped. Interview the young widow, and see if she wouldn't gladly call back the days when she was 'submissive, dependent, and childlike, in her husband's shadow.' "

Although Friedan was urging American women to work for independence and develop healthier marriages, her own marriage had been tumultuous for years. She and Carl argued in front of friends, and the physical violence between them was no secret—Friedan sometimes had black eyes. Carl once threw a bowl of sugar at her; he bore a scar from a mirror she had hurled at him. Their relationship had become especially grim during the last year that Friedan worked on her book. Carl would often stay away from their home.

After the book was published, the Friedans sold their house in Rockland County, moved to an apartment in

WHAT KIND OF WOMAN ARE YOU?

FRANTIC COOK?

Chauffeur?

Smothered Mother?

TOO INVOLVED?

Restless?

Interesting?

Informed?

Responsible Parent?

Motivated?

Satisfied?

BETTY FRIEDAN
author, "THE FEMININE MYSTIQUE"

Betty Friedan will help you decide when she speaks on

"A NEW IMAGE OF WOMAN"

Attend Temple Emanu-El Sisterhood

DONOR LUNCHEON

Tuesday, October 29, 1963

Sherry - 11:30 a.m.   Luncheon - 12:15 p.m.

Eager to spread her feminist message to women across America, Friedan actively promoted The Feminine Mystique *at a variety of events, including this speaking engagement at a women's group luncheon shortly after the book's publication.*

Manhattan, and bought a summer house in Lonelyville, Fire Island. By this time, 1963, 15-year-old Daniel, a precocious student, was already a freshman at Princeton. Jonathan, 11, and Emily, 7, were enrolled at Dalton, a prestigious private school in Manhattan. Within a few years, the family moved again, to an apartment in the Dakota building on Central Park West.

The success of *The Feminine Mystique* brought interest in a second book and a hefty advance. Friedan had an unformed idea of writing about the pattern of women's lives. Unfortunately, nothing ever came from this idea, and by the time she was supposed to return the advance money, she had spent it.

Despite these family and business problems, Friedan found strength and inspiration in her travels and speaking engagements. She was heartened in her determination to bring to light the problematic status of and attitude toward American women as more and more women confided in her and told her of their travails trying to create an identity and career in a male-dominated society.

The Feminine Mystique went on to reach more than 3 million readers and was translated into 13 languages. Its impact on the lives of women around the world was enormous—and one of the women whose life changed most was its author. The stories Friedan heard from readers propelled her into action that took her from the book review pages to the front pages of newspapers across America and around the world.

A common sight in the late 1960s, after she founded NOW: Friedan speaks out at a rally in support of equal rights for women.

FIVE

NOW

Αs Betty Friedan learned more and more about women's struggle for equality, she discovered that the Equal Employment Opportunity Commission (EEOC), a federal agency empowered by the Civil Rights Act of 1964 to end race and gender discrimination in the workplace, was concentrating on stopping racial discrimination but was doing very little to help women. The commission began its work on July 2, 1965, and within months, the few women who worked for the EEOC met opposition from their employers when they tried to take action against sex discrimination. Richard Graham, an EEOC employee who was sympathetic to the fight for women's equality, told Friedan privately that if women wanted the EEOC to work for them, they needed to

organize a group to exert political pressure on the commission. Everyone to whom Friedan spoke urged her to form such a pressure group.

Muriel Fox, a public relations executive, sent her a note saying, "If you ever decide to start an NAACP for women, count me in." (NAACP is the acronym of the National Association for the Advancement of Colored People, an organization that has been active in the battle for racial equality since 1909.) Friedan did not respond eagerly to these calls for leadership, protesting, "I'm an author. I'm not an organization person. I don't even like organizations."

But matters soon changed. In June 1966, Friedan attended a conference of state EEOC officials in Washington, D.C. She and some of the women she had met during her speaking engagements planned to try to convince someone at the conference to start a national group.

One day during the proceedings, Friedan was taken aback when a female EEOC lawyer asked to speak with her, closed her office door, and started to cry. "Mrs. Friedan," she said, "you're the only one who can do it. You have to start an NAACP for women." The lawyer's sincerity and despair made Friedan rethink her reluctance to organize.

The last evening of the conference, about 25 women packed into Friedan's tiny hotel room to discuss issues on which they could take action. One of the most egregious examples of discrimination appeared in every daily paper and severely affected women's ability to earn money: Help-wanted advertisements were divided into male and female categories. Most of the professional, well-paying jobs appeared in the column headed Male Help Wanted; the low-paying clerical and secretarial jobs that promised little chance for advancement were in the Female Help Wanted listings. All of the women in Friedan's room agreed that newspapers must stop this practice. They felt that the federal government, through the EEOC, ought to rule against these segregated advertisements, just as it had forbidden employers to discriminate against blacks by advertising for whites only. They disagreed only on what was the most effective method of pressuring the newspapers to change.

Tall, patrician Kay Clarenbach, a women's leader from Wisconsin, argued for working within the EEOC system. Friedan and the other women felt that working with the EEOC was futile. They wanted to act on their own and start a new organization, which would stage pickets outside newspaper buildings and attract media attention to force newspapers to comply with their demands. Friedan and Nancy Knaak, a friend of Clarenbach's, got into a shouting match. The argument ended when Friedan stormed into the bathroom and shut the door.

The next day, June 29, 1966, Clarenbach went to see several EEOC executives to enlist their support to end the separation of help-wanted advertisements. To her surprise, they refused. Clarenbach realized that Friedan and the others had been right. Whether because of limited funds or limited views, the opening shots in the battle against discrimination would not come from the EEOC.

As the conference came to an end, Clarenbach and the other women agreed to organize a pressure group immediately. During a lunch meeting at the Washington Hilton Hotel, while government officials delivered their closing speeches, Friedan, Clarenbach, and the others passed notes to each other and excitedly organized a group. Labor leader Catherine Conroy threw five dollars on the table to begin a treasury fund and other women, following her lead, also contributed. Their first treasury held $135.

Friedan with fellow women's rights activist Kay Clarenbach at NOW's second annual conference, which was held in November 1967. At this summit, Friedan introduced the Bill of Rights for Women, *a document that summarized NOW's goals.*

Friedan sat uncharacteristically quiet for a while, scribbling on a napkin. At last, she read aloud to the others the core of the statement of purpose for their new organization: "To take the actions needed to bring women into the mainstream of American society, now, full equality for women, in fully equal partnership with men." The group would be called NOW: the National Organization for Women—*for* not *of* women, because they did not wish to exclude men. Their hastily drawn plan became a historic landmark in the women's rights movement and a statement of feminist goals.

Friedan returned to New York City, where she and other women began recruiting NOW members. They soon had 300 members, 10 percent of whom were men. Early members included television anchorwoman Marlene Sanders, consumer reporter Betty Furness, Barnard professor (and soon-to-be feminist activist) Kate Millet, and Muriel Fox. Friedan announced the official formation of NOW at a press conference at her apartment in the Dakota on October 29, 1966. She was president; Clarenbach was chairman; Aileen Hernandez and Richard Graham were vice presidents; Caroline Davis, director of the women's department of the United Auto Workers union, was secretary treasurer.

They decided their first mission was to attack discrimination in employment. In 1966, they chose two specific targets. First, they wanted to force the EEOC to issue a ruling against separate male and female help-wanted advertisements; second, they wanted the EEOC to issue rulings protecting the jobs of airline stewardesses, who had to adhere to strict guidelines regarding their physical appearance in order to remain employed and were commonly forced to retire when they married or reached their thirties. Friedan realized "how much money the airlines saved, having all those women resign at thirty or thirty-five or marriage—how much money in raises, pensions, vacations, Social Security. Sex discrimination *was* big business." When Congress conducted hearings on the issue, outraged Congresswoman Martha Griffiths told airline executives, "If you are trying to run a whorehouse in the sky, then get a license."

Airline stewardesses march outside the White House in Washington, D.C., in protest of regulations that forced them to retire from their job if they bore children. Eliminating discrimination against women in the workplace was one of NOW's initial goals.

To make legislatures hold such hearings about the issues NOW raised, members picketed regional EEOC offices around the country. Throughout the spring of 1967, NOW members formed task forces to define specific goals of the organization in several areas of law and society.

Perhaps NOW's most urgent goal was to force employers to stop discrimination against women in the workplace. Employers should consider them for every job for which they were qualified, regardless of whether or not a woman had ever held such a position before, and adhere to the rule of equal pay for equal work.

Another vital legal and economic goal of NOW was making laws regarding marriage and divorce equitable for both parties. Marriage often meant a loss of personal rights for women. At the time, a wife could not dispose of her own property without her husband's consent. In some states, a married woman needed her husband's permission before she could serve on a jury; other states excluded women altogether. All too often, married women could not obtain credit card accounts of their own.

Research by NOW members revealed that divorce laws also affected women adversely. For instance, most women's income dropped drastically after they were divorced, while men's income often increased, for the work that a wife did was unpaid, even though it may have contributed to her husband's financial success. Because relatively few women had an employment history (and most of those who did had held only low-paying, temporary jobs), when divorced women became older they received small Social Security payments and had no stake in pension plans. Because women had little or no financial identity of their own, divorce could be economically crippling: Married adult women had no credit rating, and sometimes they were not even entitled to part of the proceeds from the sale of their own home because the deed or the mortgage was in only their husband's name.

NOW also fought to ensure that the next generation of women would grow to maturity in an atmosphere of equality. The organization demanded that school and college funds for girls be increased to reach parity with funds for boys. NOW lobbied for federal legislation that would require colleges to set up sports scholarships for girls. Controversy erupted when it petitioned politicians and school boards to allow qualified girls to play on Little League teams and other sports teams.

Textbooks deeply affect children's outlook, and NOW urged parents, teachers, and educational writers to be aware of male and female stereotypes in books for young readers. NOW felt that parents should protest against the use of such books. Instead, they and educators should choose—and write—books that present men and women as equals.

Another target in NOW's campaign was television, which was a male-dominated field. Discrimination in the television industry was visible on every nightly news show. Whereas men could keep their jobs as newscasters for decades, women were forced out as soon as they showed signs of age. In addition, few women worked in television production, and fewer still were network executives. NOW pressured the networks to hire more women in every capacity.

Finding a position on the extremely sensitive issue of reproductive freedom troubled Friedan and other NOW leaders at the organization's inception. For a long time, Friedan completely avoided the issue of abortion. She felt the best course for NOW to follow was to keep focused on employment opportunities for women and their status in public life. Taking issue with women's private lives, she thought, would divide women's solidarity.

But many people disagreed. Even though abortion was still illegal in the late 1960s, approximately 700,000 women every year had one. Most reputable doctors would not perform abortions—even if they wanted to help their patients—for fear of going to jail and losing their license. The doctors willing to perform them were often greedy, shoddy practitioners.

Back in the 1940s, when some of her friends had wanted to terminate their pregnancies, Friedan had, she said later, "personally accompanied several of these friends to scary, butchery rooms, and shared their fear and distrust of the shifty, oily, illegal operators, and sat outside the room and heard the screams and wondered what I'd do if they died, and got them into taxis afterward."

Poor women suffered most of all; because unscrupulous but competent physicians charged very high prices for an abortion, the poor could often afford only incompetent and extremely dangerous treatment. Many women died or were unable to bear children after such procedures.

Then, as now, abortion was a controversial issue. Yet the majority of NOW members felt that every woman should be allowed to decide for herself if and when she should bear children. To their way of thinking, abortion had to be legalized to ensure both freedom of choice—pro choice, as the position is often called—and medical safety.

When Friedan realized that this position was the consensus among NOW members, she threw her support behind the issue. In 1967, at the second annual convention of NOW, she presented a Bill of Rights for women that included a demand that abortions be legalized. Although some NOW members resigned in protest over Friedan's bill, the demand was added to NOW's agenda. The organization's members rejoiced six years later, on January 22, 1973, when the U.S. Supreme Court, in its decision in the case of *Roe v. Wade*, said it was illegal for individual states to restrict a woman's right to end her pregnancy in the first three months of her term.

In general, NOW members supported advances in birth control technology and convenient access to birth control, for reproductive freedom played a crucial part in the success of the women's movement. The birth control pill, a

A vice-president of NOW, Jacqui Ceballos (front row, left) was one of Friedan's earliest and staunchest allies.

highly effective and very convenient method of preventing conception, became available to American women in 1960. By the late 1960s, 8 million American women were using it.

The pill had a tremendous impact on the lives of many women. For the first time in history, they had a consistently dependable way to plan if and when they would have children. They could finish school or pursue artistic or professional careers before or after having a family. In addition, a woman could enter a career without worrying that an unwanted pregnancy would curtail her future, and educators could no longer suggest that it was more important to teach boys than girls because the latter

would inevitably become mothers and housewives.

To support such issues as reproductive freedom, equal opportunity and education, and fair marriage and divorce laws, NOW members lobbied in Washington, D.C., drew up petitions, and picketed government agencies. Most of the organization's members worked for free, often spending their own money for travel and expenses. NOW was not very organized in the beginning, and its members operated in small, makeshift offices around the country.

Under these stressful conditions, Friedan's habit of barking orders over the phone alienated many of the people

A persistent lobbyist, Friedan helped NOW gain its first major victory by convincing a federal agency, the Equal Employment Opportunity Commission, to ban the use of segregated male and female help-wanted advertisements.

she worked with in NOW. Dolores Alexander, a reporter for *Newsday*, recalled, "She would just start yelling. If she didn't approve of what we were saying or doing, her voice would rise and she'd start talking a mile a minute, abusing people. Everything was an issue for Betty. The way a meeting was run, the way a press conference was run, any plans you might be forming. She'd yell, 'No, no, no, you can't do it this way, it's gotta be done this way.' Her way. And God help us if we didn't do it that way."

Another NOW colleague, Jacqui Ceballos, recalled, "Betty's greatest strength—her aggressiveness—is also her greatest weakness. In those days it was needed; Betty was needed to completely dominate meetings, to get something accomplished."

Difficulties within NOW were not the only problems these early leaders confronted. Friedan, who lectured all over the country, often faced public ridicule and threats of bodily harm. When she gave speeches, the audience sometimes responded with derisive catcalls; she and other leaders received abusive phone calls. She once had to cancel a speaking engagement in Minnesota because of a bomb threat. Yet Friedan and the others persevered, and in 1967–68, NOW achieved its first major victory.

In 1967, the EEOC finally ruled that segregated male and female help-wanted advertisements were discriminatory. The American Newspaper Publishers Association immediately countered with a lawsuit in which the association referred to NOW as a "minuscule group of no consequence." Undeterred, Friedan and her co-workers held several fruitless meetings with executives at the *New York Times*, trying to convince them to publish sex-blind help-wanted advertisements. To bring home their point, NOW members and supporters picketed outside the Times building in Times Square for an entire year.

On December 1, 1968, the *New York Times* agreed to stop publishing help-wanted advertisements separated by gender. Before long, every newspaper in the country did the same. Exhilarated by their first success, Friedan and NOW prepared to face the larger obstacles and years of work that lay ahead.

In the 1970s, participants in the women's movement became more vocal as they took to the streets in increasing numbers to publicize their demands.

SIX

Political Action

In the late 1960s and early 1970s, as black Americans continued their fight for civil rights and public protests against the Vietnam War grew more vocal, the struggle for women's liberation became part of a nationwide upsurge of political and social activism. The Civil Rights Act of 1964, which made it illegal to discriminate against people on the basis of race (and led to the creation of the EEOC), was a direct result of activism by blacks from all walks of life, college students, and others. Student groups were also a driving force behind the anti–Vietnam War movement, and they raised public awareness of their position by staging dramatic demonstrations, rallies, and takeovers of buildings on college campuses throughout the nation.

Whenever these groups organized an event such as a rally or a march, they called newspapers and television stations to inform the media that they were about to do something dramatic and newsworthy. In this way, they were able to make a growing number of Americans aware of their goals. Some of the women who joined NOW and other feminist groups first became politically aware when they involved themselves in these other struggles, and they brought their knowledge of public demonstrations to the women's rights movement.

By late 1968, various factions of the women's movement were practicing these tactics. In the fall of that year, Robin Moore, an activist who had been a child television star, organized 200 feminists to protest outside the Miss America Pageant in Atlantic City, New Jersey. These women considered the contest, which was broadcast to millions of American homes, highly offensive because it judged women mostly by their appearance, as though they were aesthetic objects rather than actual people.

In addition to carrying signs with such slogans as Welcome to the Miss America Cattle Auction, the protesters attracted television cameras with a number of attention-getting acts. They set up a "Freedom Trash Can," into which they threw false eyelashes, girdles, dish cloths, copies of *Playboy* magazine, and other items they felt symbolized women's oppression. (The derisive term *bra burners*, referring to feminists, who were also called "women's libbers," probably dates from this event, although no one actually burned a bra at the protest.) Inside the hall, one activist interrupted the contest by throwing a stink bomb into the audience, and just as the winner was crowned, two disguised protesters in the audience disrupted the ceremony, yelling, "Down with Miss America!" as they unfurled a huge banner that read Women's Liberation. They were immediately arrested. Feminist lawyer Flo Kennedy went to the police station to help bail them out amid the chaotic, circuslike atmosphere engendered by the media. She wrote later, "It was the best fun I can imagine anyone wanting to have on any single day of her life."

The Miss America protest successfully publicized the women's move-ment throughout the country. It also established to Americans who had only a sketchy familiarity with the movement that NOW was not the only group of ardent feminists. "I admired the flair of the young radicals," Friedan said of the Atlantic City protesters.

Several months later, on February 12, 1969, Friedan and NOW organized a highly publicized event of their own—a sit-in—to help raise public consciousness about sexism (as they termed discrimination against women). Their target was the Oak Room at the Plaza Hotel in New York City, which for the past 61 years had been excluding women on weekdays from noon to three. During these hours, male executives, having the restaurant all to themselves, would talk business and make deals over lunch; their female colleagues were, in effect, barred from these meetings. The practice of sexual segregation left the women feeling not only excluded but humiliated and demoralized.

Today, it may be hard to imagine a female being turned away from a public restaurant because of her sex. But in 1969 the practice was still common, even though five years earlier the U.S. Supreme Court ruled that no public facility could refuse service to anyone on the basis of their race or sex. Nevertheless, many other restaurants, pubs, and bars across the country besides the Oak Room routinely flouted this law.

NOW scheduled the sit-in to take place on Abraham Lincoln's birthday because it wanted the public to draw a

Many of the young women who became politically active in the 1960s by taking part in the anti–Vietnam War movement later joined the women's movement, to which they brought a fiery brand of activism and the knowledge of how to stage mass demonstrations.

connection between the president's Emancipation Proclamation, which was issued to bring an end to slavery more than a century earlier, and the campaign to stop discrimination against women. Dozens of feminists attended the event, along with about 60 members of the press. All three television networks sent reporters to cover the story, as did daily newspapers, the wire services, and the foreign press.

Friedan was nearly late in arriving, but it was not because she had lost track of the time. She was reluctant to appear at the protest because she was sporting a black eye she had received during a fight with her husband. More and more, the constant battles with Carl made her think about divorcing him. But two concerns held her back. She feared that a divorce would reflect badly on the women's movement— opponents would suggest that feminism contributes to the breaking up of a marriage. And she was afraid of being alone. Friedan considers it one of the greatest ironies of her life that while she was leading the women of America to liberation, she was so dependent on her husband that she could not free herself from their destructive marriage.

On the morning of the Oak Room demonstration, Friedan had phoned her friend Dolores Alexander, who had done most of the organizing for the event, and told her she could not attend: It would not do for the president of NOW to appear at a major demonstration with a badly bruised eye ob-

tained during a domestic squabble. Alexander thought quickly and contacted Jean Faust, the president of NOW's New York chapter and formerly a theater makeup artist. Faust raced over to Friedan's apartment and applied heavy makeup to Friedan's eye to cover the discoloration. Friedan arrived at the Plaza exactly at noon, just in time to join the demonstrators.

While the press corps filled the hall outside the Oak Room, the women filed into the restaurant. As they expected, the maître d'hôtel stopped them at the door. "We have the Edwardian Room for you ladies," he told them. "It's a beautiful restaurant." "That's separate and unequal," the protesters retorted as they pushed past him into the Oak Room and sat down at the tables. They called for service— in vain, as it turned out; the waiters were under orders not to serve them. The demonstrators remained in the Oak Room for half an hour without being waited on. Then they left, convinced that they had drawn attention to their demand.

Not all the attention was positive, however. In the following day's *New York Post*, columnist Harriet Van Horne wrote derisively, "For a woman to stroll into a men's bar at lunchtime and demand service seems to be as preposterous as a woman marching into a barbershop and demanding a hot towel and a haircut. . . . This storming of the Oak Room was . . . a shrewish, attention-seeking stunt. . . . Women lose so much—beginning with charm, dignity and a certain mystery—when they carry on like strumpets in foolish causes."

Another journalist who covered the sit-in at the Oak Room was Gloria Steinem, who at the time wrote for *New York* magazine. Her enthusiastic response to the event was quite different from Van Horne's. Shortly after the protest, she became involved in the feminists' struggle for equal rights, and she soon emerged as a leading spokesperson for the movement.

In the following decade, Steinem and Friedan often appeared jointly at events in support of the women's movement. But over time the two women grew to be bitter rivals. Steinem, 10 years younger than Friedan, was tall, thin, and glamorous; she was also witty and cooperated with the press. Friedan, on the other hand, was known for being imperious and abrasive. Steinem quickly became one of the media's favorite feminists, while Friedan lost favor with reporters.

Soon after the Oak Room demonstration, Friedan was invited to speak at a conference in Zurich, Switzerland. She planned to go by herself, despite her

Flo Kennedy's taste for flamboyant outfits made her one of the most recognizable spokespersons for the women's rights movement. A prominent lawyer, she helped bail out the feminists who were jailed for holding a public protest against the 1968 Miss America Pageant.

In the 1970s, the call to legalize abortion became one of the leading issues of the women's rights movement.

fear of loneliness, which was intensified because she had never before been to Europe. She decided that if she could manage to travel alone to Zurich and then go on to Paris and Rome and not fall apart emotionally, she could find the courage to divorce her husband. Her trip went well—she proved to herself that she could function alone—and upon her return to New York she told Carl she wanted to end their marriage. They filed for divorce in Mexico in May 1969.

On the day of the divorce decree, Friedan recalled, "I went to a bar and sat and cried, not because I was alone but for all the wasted years." Carl confirmed her fears about adverse publicity by announcing to the press, "She hates men. Let's face it, they all do—all those activists in the women's lib movement. I've seen 'em traipse through my living room."

Among the NOW leaders traipsing through each other's living room in 1969 were Bella Abzug, Flo Kennedy, and Ti-Grace Atkinson. Abzug, a lawyer and outspoken politician from the borough of the Bronx in New York City, worked closely with Friedan throughout the late 1960s. Great animosity developed between them, however, when Abzug became a close ally of Steinem's. The 53-year-old Kennedy, a flamboyant lawyer from Kansas City, Missouri, was known for defending prominent black musicians and civil rights activists, including vocalist Billie Holiday, saxophonist Charlie Parker, and the militant H. Rap Brown. Her friend Ti-Grace Atkinson, a tall, blond Louisianan, was chosen by Friedan to be the president of the New

York chapter of NOW in 1968. But Atkinson was far more radical than most of the NOW women and fond of making impulsive, sometimes outrageous comments to the press.

These women had somewhat different goals. Kennedy and Atkinson, for instance, advocated a revolutionary restructuring of society, whereas Friedan had conceived NOW's original purpose as helping women operate within the mainstream of American culture. Nevertheless, these feminists were all united in their desire to free women from the limited expectations and opportunities of the past and to pressure the government to protect their rights as equal citizens.

69

Each had her own style and tactics. Atkinson once proclaimed to the *New York Times*, "The institution of marriage has the same effect as the institution of slavery." Friedan feared that such provocative comments would antagonize most Americans and repel them from the women's movement. When the controversial pop artist Andy Warhol was shot by a disturbed woman named Valeria Solanis, Atkinson shocked Friedan and her NOW colleagues by speaking out in Solanis's support and asking Flo Kennedy to be Solanis's lawyer. Friedan immediately sent Kennedy a telegram: "Desist immediately from linking the National Organization for Women in any way with the case of Valeria Solanis. Miss Solanis' motives in the Warhol case are entirely irrelevant to NOW's goals." Eventually, Kennedy and Atkinson left NOW and formed a more radical group called the Feminists.

One group that Friedan felt particularly threatened by was the increasingly vocal lesbian contingent within the women's rights movement. Friedan always resisted linking lesbianism with feminism. She felt that sexual preference was a private matter, not a political one. She also felt that if NOW became associated with lesbians, the organization's reputation among the majority of Americans would suffer— lesbianism was not widely approved of in most layers of society—and potential members and sources of support might be frightened away.

Friedan's refusal to include lesbian issues on NOW's agenda led to a serious rift in the movement. Lesbian groups derided NOW as being composed of the four M's: "Middle-class, middle-aged, moderate matrons." For her part, Friedan knew it was impossible to support the demands of every feminist. Yet she did not want a splintering of the women's rights movement. A united campaign, she knew, could wield considerable political power.

Consequently, Friedan's call for a March for Equality on August 26, 1970, was in part a cry for renewed cohesion among the movement's various factions. But it was not an easy task to rally the troops. Her popularity among feminists was on the wane, especially among her co-workers in NOW, who objected to her often abrasive managerial style.

"To transmit this new vision to the [1970] NOW convention in Chicago, warning of the dangers of aborting the women's movement, I spoke for nearly two hours," Friedan recalled. She received a standing ovation for her rousing speech. And, much to her relief, the massive march proved to be a great success. "On August 26," she claimed, "it suddenly became both political and glamorous to be a feminist."

Shortly thereafter, Friedan began to work on organizing a women's political caucus. But on December 12, 1970, a familiar divisive issue regained the spotlight. On that day, Friedan braved a sleet storm in New York to join several thousand women in a march on Gracie Mansion, the mayor's residence, to demand more financial support for child-

A prominent figure in the women's rights movement, Barnard College professor Kate Millet (left) wrote the deeply influential Sexual Politics, *an analysis of the portrayal of women in literature.*

care centers and legal abortions. Friedan, Steinem, Kennedy, and Kate Millet, who were slated to give speeches, mounted a flatbed truck. Meanwhile, Ivy Bottini, president of the New York chapter of NOW, and other women started handing out lavender (the color that lesbians have chosen as their symbol) armbands for every marcher to wear, along with leaflets that read, "It is not one woman's sexual experience that is under attack—it is the freedom of all women to openly state values that fundamentally challenge the basic structure of patriarchy.

If they succeed in scaring us with words like 'dyke' or 'lesbian' or 'bisexual,' they'll have won. AGAIN. They'll have divided us. . . . They can call us all lesbians until such time as there is no stigma attached to women loving women. SISTERHOOD IS POWERFUL!"

Friedan was shocked that Bottini and other women's rights leaders were equating feminism with lesbianism, and she was furious that she had been asked to lend her name to the march without having been informed of their overall plan. Bottini gave Friedan a lav-

71

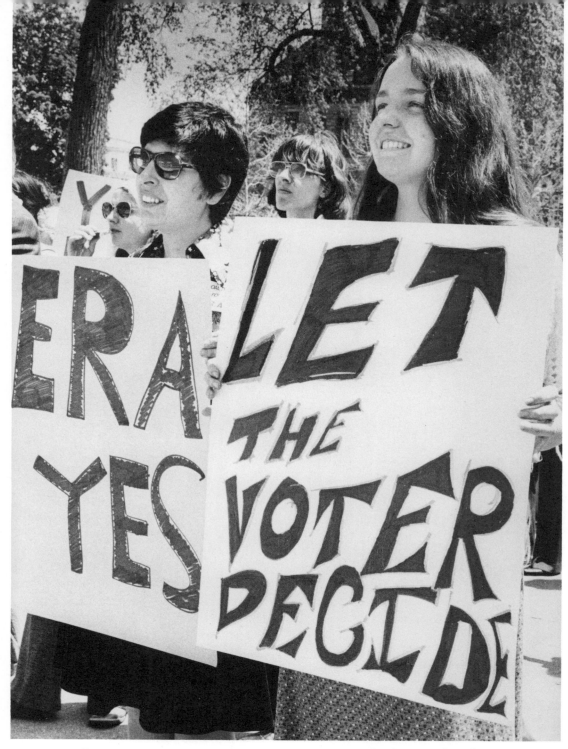

In an attempt to get state governments to ratify the Equal Rights Amendment and make it part of the U.S. Constitution, women picketed outside state legislatures through much of the 1970s.

ender armband and watched her drop it to the floor of the flatbed truck. After the rally, Friedan, Millet, and others went to a nearby bar, where Friedan learned that Steinem and many of the other feminist leaders were planning to declare in a press conference, "We are all lesbians." In her 1976 anthology *It Changed My Life*, Friedan wrote, "I begged them not to do it. I said the women's movement was too important to too many people who were not necessarily lesbians. . . . In fact, that sexual red herring of lesbianism did preoccupy and divide—or was used and manipulated to divide—NOW and the women's movement for months, for years thereafter."

Despite these problems, Friedan continued to struggle to make the women's rights movement an influential political force that would achieve the feminists' legislative goals. She convened the first National Women's Political Caucus in 1971, which helped elect Bella Abzug to Congress. One

year later, the women's caucus joined the battle to add to the U.S. Constitution the Equal Rights Amendment (ERA), which had originally been introduced in Congress in 1923. The 1972 version of the proposed amendment read in full:

> Section 1. Equality of rights under the law shall not be denied or abridged by the United States or by any State on account of sex.
> Section 2. The congress shall have the power to enforce, by appropriate legislation, the provisions of this article.

Although Congress ratified the amendment in 1972, this action was not sufficient to make it a part of the Constitution. In addition, 38 state legislatures (two-thirds of the total number of states) had to approve the ERA for it to be adopted. The struggle to have the ERA ratified continued over the next decade—an era of great change in the United States, the women's rights movement, and Friedan's life.

Although Friedan stepped down from the presidency of NOW at the beginning of the 1970s, she continued her efforts throughout the decade to get the Equal Rights Amendment ratified.

SEVEN

"It Changed My Life"

In the 1970s, feminists began to realize their goals as the status of American women changed greatly. Police and fire departments around the country allowed qualified women to join their ranks. Major corporations and small companies alike, including AT&T, Sears, Roebuck and Company, and the *New York Times*, started to hire more women, as well as train and promote them to skilled and managerial jobs—at first to avoid or settle lawsuits, and later because they began to appreciate the potential of the female labor force.

Improved opportunities attracted a growing number of women to pursue careers. In 1963, the year *The Feminine Mystique* was published, 38 percent of American women were working. By 1981, 52 percent were employed.

Women also began to attend professional schools in increasing numbers. Between 1970 and 1979, the percentage of law school graduates who were women jumped from 5.4 to 28.5, a rise of nearly 500 percent. Among medical school graduates, the percentage increase was nearly as great, from 8.4 to 23.0.

Women made gains in the field of politics and in the courts. They became pages in the Senate, formerly an honor reserved for young men. In 1974, Ella Grasso of Connecticut became the first female governor to be elected in her own right (not as a widow or wife of a previous governor). NOW members rejoiced when laws were passed that made it illegal for banks to deny a married woman her own credit card.

Newly adopted legislation also made it possible for a woman who is raped by her husband to charge him with the crime.

Changes in language reflected not only how women were being perceived and treated but how they felt about themselves. More and more women began keeping their own last name when they married, instead of taking their husband's surname. The title *Ms.*, a form of address that identifies a woman without indicating the absence or presence of a husband (as Miss and Mrs. do), became part of the language. So did the word *sexist*, which was used in a derogatory manner. Many people also considered it unacceptable for grown women to be called "girls." Indeed, a large number of Americans became aware of the implications of the words they used to identify men and women.

The most dramatic changes of all took place in the domestic lives of men and women. Men shared housework with their wives more than they ever had. They also helped raise their children to a greater degree than ever before. Young fathers carried their newborn babies in backpacks, took them to parks, learned how to bathe and dress and soothe them. These were significant changes, for previous generations of men had grown up in households where the mother—never the father—did the laundry, made the beds, washed the dishes, and picked up after the children.

Not surprisingly, for women who were brought up to be dependent on men and who were taught to let men make their decisions, it was very difficult to suddenly take responsibility for their own life. Friedan wrote in 1976, "The whole story is clearly more than a few women reversing roles with men or having a piece of the action, a chance at the jobs only men had before. Something else begins to happen—a bridging, a transcending of the polarization between masculine and feminine, between the abstract and concrete, between eternal values and grubby, sweaty, everyday realities. It will not be a separate story very long. The rights were won after a century of struggle, and then there was a half-century of sleep, and now the women's movement is changing society so women can use those rights. And then it will be human liberation."

Friedan was proud of her efforts to bring about this revolution, although her role as president of NOW had come to an end early in the decade. Personality conflicts and political disagreements had plagued the women's movement and deeply affected Friedan's ability to get things done. In 1970, she stepped down from her post as president of NOW. Lucy Kamisar, a NOW vice-president who worked with Friedan, told the *New York Times*, "There just isn't a place for her in an ongoing organization like ours."

Most activists knew Friedan had been effectively forced out of the NOW leadership. Even though she was allowed to retain the title of chairperson of the organization's advisory committee (she kept the title until 1972), the

The growing political power of women was evident at the 1972 Democratic National Convention, where they made up nearly 40 percent of the delegates. Nevertheless, they were disappointed when the Democratic party's presidential candidate, George McGovern (at podium), refused to adopt the plank regarding abortion that the female delegates had proposed.

chair was essentially a powerless position. Kamisar went so far as to suggest to the *New York Times*, "There is no advisory committee."

In the summer of 1972, Friedan left the sidelines to join forces with other feminists who arrived in Miami, Florida, as delegates for the Democratic National Convention. They planned to offer their support to the party's leading presidential candidate, George McGovern, who sought the Democratic nomination in his bid for office against the Republican incumbent, Richard Nixon. An unprecedented 40 percent of the official delegates to the convention were women (only 14 percent of the delegates at the previous convention had been female), and they were eager to influence the issues (called planks) on which a presidential nominee would run his campaign.

Day after day, the female delegates gathered in meetings to discuss which issues they would ask McGovern to incorporate into his political platform. Friedan, who served as vice-president of the National Association to Repeal Abortion Laws from 1970 to 1973, hoped that the women's caucus would insist on getting McGovern to make the right to have an abortion a part of his campaign agenda. Like most people, Friedan knew that the majority of convention delegates would never agree to include such a plank and that McGovern would not strongly support legalizing abortion because he feared it would cost him too many votes in the national election. Friedan understood this, yet she and her friend Jacqui Ceballos, a former NOW vice-president, were determined to bring the issue up for debate on the convention floor, which in itself would set a precedent and represent a victory for the women's caucus. Friedan also wanted McGovern to promise the women's caucus that he would support the right to have an abortion if he were elected, even if he would not include it on his campaign agenda.

When McGovern came to speak to the women's caucus, the group greeted his arrival with a storm of enthusiastic cheers. According to Germaine Greer, a well-known feminist journalist from Australia, "He had them in the palm of his hand, he could no longer doubt it

. . . his women were a pushover. I raged inside, to think what such spontaneity and generosity would cost them."

Jacqui Ceballos, standing just below the stage, interrupted the politician's speech. "What about the right to control our own bodies?" she cried. "We'll never be free until we have that!" McGovern ignored her.

Despite McGovern's obvious reluctance to deal with the abortion issue, Friedan helped push it to the convention floor, where it was publicly discussed. In doing so, she incurred Gloria Steinem's wrath. "The night of McGovern's nomination, in the space behind the stadium bleachers at the Democratic convention in Miami, I finally came into open conflict with Gloria Steinem," Friedan said in describing their clash. "Or rather I shouted, and she said sweetly, in effect, that I had to get out or else."

The feud between Steinem and Friedan soon reached the press. Nora Ephron, commenting in *Harper's* magazine, wrote, "Gloria is not, after all, uninterested in power. And yet, she manages to remain above the feud, but that is partly because, unlike Betty, she has friends who will fight dirty for her. Still, it is hard to come out anywhere but squarely on her side. Betty Friedan, in her thoroughly irrational hatred for Steinem, has ceased caring whether or not the effects of that hatred are good or bad for the women's movement."

Feminists always had a tacit understanding that they would refrain from criticizing each other in public, in order to maintain an appearance of solidarity.

Immediately after Friedan (above) spoke out at the 1972 Democratic National Convention with the purpose of inciting the delegates to debate the issue of legalized abortion, her long-standing rivalry with feminist leader Gloria Steinem (below) turned into a highly public conflict.

Friedan bicycles down a path in the Hamptons, a resort community in Long Island, New York. To provide her with a place to relax away from her Manhattan apartment, she rented a house in the Hamptons with a group of friends during the early 1970s.

After the convention, however, Friedan publicly attacked Steinem for the first time. In a column she wrote regularly for *McCall's*, Friedan accused her of "female chauvinism." Steinem retorted, "If anyone's past actions have been female chauvinism, it's [Friedan's]."

Other feminists also condemned Friedan, claiming she had damaged the movement by criticizing Steinem in print. A wave of feeling rose up against the former NOW president. Lucy Kamisar told the *New York Times*, "The woman needs to be brought under control."

Despite her difficulties with co-workers in the movement, Friedan managed to maintain a group of friends whom she called her "extended family." During the early 1970s, they rented a house in the Hamptons, on Long Island, and spent many summers and holidays together—a "commune," Friedan half-jokingly called it. Among her friends were several influential people, including journalist Betty Rollin; writer Arthur Herzog; the eminent sociologist William J. Goode; television journalist Marlene Sanders; and the songwriters Betty Comden and Adolph Green.

Throughout the 1970s, Friedan continued to lecture and write about the women's movement. Although she lost touch with many of the women she had worked with in NOW's early days, she was still considered a spokeswoman for the movement, and she described herself as a "visionary." In 1973, she took it upon herself to request an audience with Pope Paul VI at the Vatican in Rome, in an effort to extend the influence of feminism to women around the world.

Many feminists view the pope, the spiritual leader of more than 926 million Catholics (18.5 percent of the world's population) to be an opponent of women's equality. Not only does the Roman Catholic church expressly forbid abortion as a mortal sin—even in cases in which a mother will die in her effort to complete a pregnancy—but in 1968 Pope Paul VI had also issued an encyclical (a formal letter to all bishops that clarifies church teachings) titled *Humanae Vitae* (On Human Life) that completely condemned all artificial methods of birth control. In addition, feminists took issue with the Catholic church's continuing refusal to ordain women as priests. (Although some American women claim to be priests, they have not been officially ordained by the pope.)

For his part, the pope could hardly be blamed if he viewed Friedan as an enemy. After all, she had spearheaded a movement with goals that are antithetical to Roman Catholic teaching. Friedan had worked to legalize abortion in the United States, and she believed every woman should have access to her choice of birth control.

Despite their extreme differences, Pope Paul VI agreed to grant Friedan an audience. Many Catholics who sympathized with the women's movement awaited the meeting with high expectations. Perhaps, they thought, the pope might be persuaded to relax his traditional stance on issues relating to women.

When Friedan was ushered into Pope Paul's presence, he presented her with a jewel box, saying, "We want to express our gratitude and appreciation for all you have done for the women of the world." Friedan then gave the pope a chain with a gold-plated pendant symbolizing women's equality. She said, "This is the symbol of the women's movement—the sign of the female, in biology, crossed by the sign of absolute equality . . . in the hope and expectation that the Catholic church is going to come to profound new terms with the personhood of women, and . . . will become a force for the liberation of women."

After a brief conversation, the audience was over. The Catholic church did not budge from its position, nor did Friedan. In fact, the two popes who have succeeded Paul VI—John Paul I and John Paul II—have forcefully reaffirmed the traditional Roman Catholic position of being opposed to contraception, abortion, and the ordination of women.

The Protestant and Jewish religions have been more receptive to the women's movement. Since the 1970s, some Protestant denominations in the United States, including Episcopalians and Methodists, have ordained women as ministers and even bishops. The reform branch of Judaism has also accepted women rabbis since the 1970s,

and the conservative branch has allowed them since the beginning of the 1980s.

Other attempts to make the women's movement become an international force had similarly dispiriting results. In July 1975, the United Nations sponsored an International Women's Conference in Mexico City. Even before Friedan left for Mexico, her participation in the conference created problems. She received letters warning her not to speak at the conference or she would be denounced "first as an American and then as a Jew." As soon as she arrived in Mexico, she was surrounded by controversy.

According to Friedan, delegates from some less-developed countries who perceived the United States as an imperialist power that often interfered unduly in other nations' affairs believed that American feminists, by association, were guilty of being oppressors. Delegates from China and some other countries, Friedan said, did not want American feminists, who in 1975 were among the world's more outspoken and independent women, to influence their nation's women. During the conference, Friedan and other feminists struggled to unite women from different countries to discover what goals they shared and what steps they could take to help all women.

The Mexican feminist Esperanza Marti told an audience, "They [the Mexican government] have told us in every kind of voice that we should not unite with our sisters in the developed

Friedan exchanges gifts with Pope Paul VI (left) at the Vatican in 1973. She had requested an audience with the pontiff in the hope that she could persuade him to alter his traditional stance on such issues as abortion and birth control.

countries, that they are our enemies. This is a lie."

During the time she was in Mexico, Friedan was followed, she later claimed. One day, the Mexican attorney general questioned her. Another day, a group of men disrupted the conference by shouting and marching among them, carrying a huge banner that said in Spanish: Women and Imperialism.

The American press also criticized Friedan. A *New York Post* report of the women's conference said: "American feminists are trying to head off a Latin American move to censure Betty Friedan for 'manipulative tactics.'" One American woman said after the conference, "I've been darn upset with Betty Friedan and her bulldozing tactics."

Friedan included an account of her Mexico City experiences in *It Changed My Life*, an anthology of her writing that was published in 1976. The book received a mix of laudatory and critical reviews. A reviewer in the *New York Times* said, "She has had the courage to be a middle-class extremist . . . her goal is to mobilize [women] by urging them to break out of domestic isolation. Her pragmatic gospel calls on women to win, in proportion to their numbers, policy-making positions in industry, labor unions, the churches, the educational system, the professions, the political parties." But the reviewer also said of Friedan, "She has raised politically sensational questions . . . and she has failed to spell out or document her answers."

Despite receiving criticism from both inside and outside the women's movement, Friedan continued to lecture, write, and be recognized for her achievements throughout the 1970s. She taught classes and seminars as a visiting professor of sociology at Temple University and Queens College, was a visiting lecturer and fellow at Yale University, and became a founder of the First Women's Bank and Trust Company. In 1975, the American Humanist Society named her Humanist of the Year; that same year, her alma mater, Smith College, awarded her a doctorate of humane letters.

However, the most important work that Friedan and many feminists focused on in the 1970s was the attempt to get the Equal Rights Amendment (ERA) passed. Friedan put aside her grievances with the lesbians in the women's movement in an attempt to restore feminist unity so that they could fight more powerfully for the ERA. When she spoke in 1977 at the First National Women's Conference, in Houston, Texas, it became clear that she had modified her stance. Referring to a sexual preference resolution that lesbians urged be added to the ERA, Friedan said: "I've been known to be violently opposed to the lesbian issue in the women's movement and I have been. I'm someone who grew up in Middle America, and maybe I love men too much. We have all made mistakes and we have all learned. I now see there is nothing in ERA to protect lesbians, and so I urge adoption of this measure."

An organized, united movement for

Friedan celebrates the 12th anniversary of the publication of The Feminine Mystique *by signing copies of the book for her readers.*

the ERA was necessary, for its foes were organized as well. One of the most outspoken opponents of the ERA was Phyllis Schlafly, a lawyer from St. Louis, Missouri, who founded a group called Stop ERA. She said in a debate with Friedan, "If ERA is ratified not only would women, including mothers, be subject to the draft, but the military would be compelled to place them in combat units along side of men. It could relieve the fathers of the primary responsibilities for the support of infant children as well as the support of even the mothers of such children. . . . These

are some of the reasons why I feel that the Equal Right Amendment is not the way to go. It's no way to improve the status of women. We have a wonderful position in our country today, so don't knock it."

Friedan responded, "While motherhood might be the most important fact for a woman's life during the years that she was actively a mother, and might be a most important value in her whole life, it could no longer occupy most of a woman's life and she had to confront her situation in society. And the reality of the Equal Rights Amendment, why it is needed, is that most women are going to have to spend most of their lives in some occupation in society where they are not now equal, where they are barred and have been barred from many jobs . . . from job training programs and to other necessary conditions of equal opportunity for women including maternity leaves and the like." In her writing, Friedan pointed out that Schlafly, a professional career

woman, had benefited greatly from the gains of feminism herself.

In 1977, Congress passed the Pregnancy Disability Act, giving women legal protection from being fired from their jobs because they were pregnant or had just given birth to a child. The act was a major victory for women, but it was not enough. At the end of the decade, the momentum for legislative change culminated in an intense strug-

One of Friedan's most outspoken opponents in the 1970s and 1980s was attorney Phyllis Schlafly, who founded the Stop ERA movement largely because she wanted to prevent women from being subjected to the military draft.

gle by virtually the entire women's movement, along with many labor, civic, and religious organizations, for passage of the ERA. Appending the ERA to the Constitution would make such narrowly directed legislation as the Pregnancy Disability Act unnecessary because the amendment would forbid any discrimination on the basis of sex.

The ERA was supported by 450 organizations representing 50 million Americans. It was ratified by 35 out of the 38 necessary states. Women in the Democratic party scored a long-sought victory in August 1980 at the Demo-cratic National Convention in New York City when they finally turned support for the ERA into a plank in Jimmy Carter's reelection platform (over the candidate's objections).

But the much-awaited victory never came. Despite the fervent push for adoption of the ERA by Friedan, Steinem, NOW, *Ms.* magazine, Representative Martha Griffiths (who originally forced it out of committee to the House floor for the first time since 1948), and by women and men around the country, the amendment remained 3 state votes short of passage by the deadline of June 30, 1982.

Friedan opens an account at the First Women's Bank in New York City, a savings and loan institution run chiefly by and for women. She has always believed that economic equality is one of the most important goals of feminism.

EIGHT

The Second Stage

The defeat of the Equal Rights Amendment prompted some social scientists and commentators to declare that the women's movement was in decline. They said that many women had lost interest in agitating for equal rights because the movement had already served its purpose. As proof, they pointed out that women had begun to make inroads into fields that had long been dominated by males: In 1981, Sandra Day O'Connor became the first woman appointed to the Supreme Court; in 1983, Sally Ride became the first American woman to travel in space; and in 1984, Geraldine Ferraro was the first female vice-presidential nominee.

In spite of these breakthroughs, serious inequalities between the two sexes still persisted. Throughout the early 1980s, for every dollar earned by the average man, the average woman earned around 68 cents. In 1986, wives working full-time averaged $13,070, far less than the $23,800 earned by working husbands.

In many states, divorce laws have been changed to give men and women equal status. Nevertheless, after a divorce a woman's income generally drops to 73 percent less than what it had been previously. Women and children make up 93 percent of all welfare recipients in the nation, and women head 80 percent of the families that receive Aid to Families with Dependent Children, a federal subsidy.

In 1980, Friedan served as a delegate to the White House Conference on

Families, whose purpose was to investigate the makeup of different types of households around the country. The 1980 census revealed that only the husband worked for a living in 11 percent of the families that consisted of a husband, wife, and children; both the husband and the wife worked in 21 percent of the families that were made up of them and their children. Consequently, less than one-third of the American population lived in what had once been considered a traditional family (two parents living with their offspring).

Struck by how many single mothers struggled to combine work outside the home with the responsibilities of motherhood, Friedan rethought some of the goals of the women's movement. In *The Second Stage*, which was published in 1981, she discussed her active participation in the White House Conference on Families, addressed the evolution of feminism, and qualified some of the stances she had adopted in *The Feminine Mystique*. When the movement was at its peak, she said in *The Second Stage*, the family became neglected; as women surged into the workforce, they often postponed marriage and child bearing. As the years passed, however, she had met a number of successful women who told her how deeply they regretted not having taken the time to have children.

Friedan did not repudiate the basic feminist principles she had helped formulate two decades earlier. Nor did she embrace the calls of some traditionalists who urged a return to the unequal roles of the past. "The millions of women," she wrote, "who take themselves seriously as people now and take for granted their entitlement to equal rights—even if they say they are not feminists, disapprove of feminists, feel threatened by feminists, are closet feminists, or are still unconscious of their own feminist fire—are not going to turn into bland plastic robots, à la Stepford Wives, or Doris Day simpering housewives overnight."

Friedan felt that many opponents of the women's movement were quick to claim that they were trying to save the family unit. In addition, they tried to categorize all feminists as being opposed to family life. Family life and feminist values were not in opposition, Friedan argued. Rather, contemporary society made it extremely difficult to make ends meet and to keep the family together. The way many jobs and careers were set up, a person needed to have full-time, unpaid domestic help to make it all work out.

But in *The Second Stage* Friedan also criticized the women's movement. In fact, the book aroused a storm of controversy, much of which centered on her attitude toward sexual politics. "In the second stage, the women's movement directed too much of its energy into sexual politics," she wrote. "From personal bedroom wars against men to mass marches against rape or pornography to 'take back the night.' . . . Sexual war against men is an irrelevant, self-defeating acting out of rage. It does not change the conditions of our lives. Obsession with rape, even offering Band-Aids to its victims, is a kind of

Friedan appears at a rally during NOW's 10th annual convention, which was held in Detroit, Michigan, in 1977. She continued to appear regularly throughout the 1980s at events sponsored by NOW.

wallowing in the victim state, that impotent rage, that sterile polarization."

Friedan outraged many feminists with her comments about victims of rape. The *New York Times* reviewer wrote, "Oddly, Miss Friedan blames the victim." The French feminist author Simone de Beauvoir, author of *The Second Sex*, said that Friedan's book annoyed her so much she threw it across the room.

Friedan's preoccupation with family issues may have been influenced by her pride in her own family; she wrote *The Second Stage* at about the same time that she became a grandmother. Her son Jonathan, an engineer, is now married to a free-lance writer and has two sons. Friedan's other son, Daniel, is a theoretical physicist at the University of Chicago and has been the recipient of a MacArthur Award. Her daughter, Emily, a graduate of Harvard Medical

School, is married to a physician at the University of Buffalo Medical School and has a son. Emily, who formed a woman's group when she was a medical student at Harvard, has said of her mother, "I'm proud of what she did, and I'm reaping the benefits."

By the middle of the 1980s, many women saw Friedan as the mother of the modern feminist movement, and she continued to involve herself in its growth. During the summer of 1985, she flew to Nairobi, Kenya, for the third United Nations World Conference on Women, attended by nearly 17,000 women representing 159 countries. Although Friedan thought that activism was flagging in the United States, she listened eagerly to feminist leaders from Asia, Africa, Europe, and Latin America as they spoke of their successes in gaining a measure of equality and discussed the challenges of what remained to be done.

The conference astonished Friedan. She wrote, "It was truly humiliating to

Protesters from many nations attend a demonstration in support of abortion and birth control outside United Nations headquarters in New York City. In 1985, Friedan went to Nairobi, Kenya, to attend the third United Nations World Conference on Women, an international summit that signaled to her that the struggle for women's rights had become a worldwide phenomenon.

In 1986, Friedan joined Phineas Indritz (center) and Muriel Fox (right) in Washington, D.C., at the 20th reunion of NOW founders. That same year, Friedan also spoke at a larger anniversary celebration, which was held in Los Angeles, California.

discover that we are no longer the cutting edge of modern feminism or world progress toward equality. Even Kenya has an equal rights clause in its Constitution!" That year, sparked by what she had learned in Kenya, she wrote an article entitled "How to Get the Women's Movement Moving Again" for the widely read Sunday magazine of the *New York Times*. In the article, she asked, "How can we let the women's movement die out here in America when what we began is taking hold now all over the world?" She answered with a 10-point program addressing the

dilemmas that had left the American women's movement paralyzed. The article evoked a tremendous response and strengthened Friedan's reputation as one of feminism's leading and most controversial thinkers.

In 1986, NOW marked its 20th anniversary with a celebration at the Dorothy Chandler Pavilion in Los Angeles, California. Friedan addressed a capacity crowd during the event. "NOW went beyond our wildest dreams," she told her listeners. "Our daughters take it for granted that they will play in Little League, that they can be astronauts and that they can run for President. It broke through the barriers of explicit sex discrimination."

A year later, Friedan attended another celebration, a huge 65th birthday party her friends threw for her at New York's Palladium discotheque.

Although Friedan showed no sign of letting age slow her down, her advancing years prompted her to tackle a new subject in her writings: how senior citizens could break through society's false perceptions of aging. She had begun researching the "mystique of age," as she called it, almost 10 years earlier, and was finishing a book, tentatively titled *The Fountain of Age*, on the subject as the 1980s drew to a close. To help her along, she received funding from a grant given by the Ford Foundation and worked as a senior research associate at the Center for the Social Sciences at Columbia University.

"I think we will be finding all kinds of new patterns for love, growth, and work in that portion of life that comes after age 50," she said while doing research for the book. "I think we can fight those forces of deterioration and stagnation and decline. What the woman's movement has proven is that women, long past their so-called prime of life, can accomplish great things and grow each year in stature and creative ability. So now I'm going to devote more time to liberating older people from the limiting myths about old age."

At a 1988 New York conference called "Who Is Responsible for My Old Age?" Friedan told her audience,

"There is a denial of the personhood of age" because people cannot bear to think that they will ever be one of "those dreary, decrepit, senile, smelly, isolated, lonely, incontinent, childlike elderly. Not us," she added defiantly. "We have not even begun to study what might emerge in terms of human maturity."

She added, "If I am right, the breakthrough to new thinking about age will catalyze a new movement for social change in the last years of this century, comparable to the youth, black and women's movement of the last 25 years, breaking through the denial of age, looking at the new third of age, not as decline from the male youthful peak, but on its own terms . . . requiring new concepts of family, new concepts of intimacy, and bonding and sexuality; new concepts of work . . . new concepts of housing, education, recreation, and medical care, as well as new economic and social policies."

Friedan has already taught millions of women—and men—to understand the ideas that constrained them and thus has helped them to change themselves, as well as the laws and attitudes of America, so that women now are closer than ever to living in full equality with men. In doing so, she has fundamentally altered the course of life in America. Throughout her career, she has moved from analyzing her personal experience as a woman and as an aging American to thinking, writing, and teaching about larger public issues that affect all women and the aged. By founding NOW, and in three decades of

After almost three decades of theorizing, writing, and speaking about feminism, Friedan has turned to a new subject—discrimination against the aged.

writing, speaking, and teaching around the world, she has helped women unite to achieve common goals. Her success or failure to do the same for the aged remains to be seen, but she plans to attack the issue with her characteristic blend of incisive thought, startling conclusions, and fiery conviction.

"Neither I nor any woman could break the vicious circle alone," Friedan has said in summing up her work in the women's movement. "We found our strength by confronting the conditions that made us what we were as women, and by acting together to change them."

FURTHER READING

Cohen, Marcia. *The Sisterhood: The True Story Behind the Women's Movement.* New York: Simon & Schuster, 1988.

Daffron, Carolyn. *Gloria Steinem.* New York: Chelsea House, 1988.

Friedan, Betty. *The Feminine Mystique.* New York: Dell, 1983.

————. *It Changed My Life: Writings on the Women's Movement.* New York: Norton, 1985.

————. *The Second Stage.* New York: Summit, 1981.

Morgan, Robin, ed. *Sisterhood Is Powerful: An Anthology of Writings from the Women's Liberation Movement.* New York: Random House, 1970.

O'Neill, William L. *Everyone Was Brave: The Rise and Fall of Feminism in America.* New York: Quadrangle, 1969.

Rossi, Alice S., ed. *The Feminist Papers: From Adams to De Beauvoir.* Boston: Northeastern University Press, 1988.

CHRONOLOGY

Feb. 4, 1921	Born Elizabeth Naomi Goldstein in Peoria, Illinois
1939	Enters Smith College
1942	Graduates summa cum laude and valedictorian from Smith; wins fellowship to study at the University of California at Berkeley
1943	Moves to New York and begins working for the *Federated Press*, a labor newspaper
1947	Marries Carl Friedan
1948	Son Daniel is born
1952	Son Jonathan is born
1956	Daughter, Emily, is born
1963	*The Feminine Mystique* is published
1966	As its first president, Friedan announces the official formation of the National Organization for Women (NOW)
1967	Presents Bill of Rights for Women at the second annual convention of NOW; EEOC rules that segregated male and female help-wanted ads are discriminatory
1969	NOW activists stage a lunchtime sit-in at the Oak Room at the Plaza Hotel in New York City; Friedan and husband Carl divorce
1970	Thousands of men and women join the March for Equality in New York City; Friedan resigns as president of NOW
1971	Convenes the first National Women's Political Caucus along with other feminists
1973	Is granted an audience with Pope Paul VI
1976	*It Changed My Life* is published
1980	Friedan serves as delegate to the White House Conference on Families
1981	*The Second Stage* is published
1985	"How to Get the Women's Movement Moving Again" is published in the *New York Times*
1990	Friedan continues to lecture, research, and work on her forthcoming book about the aged in America

INDEX

INDEX

INDEX

PICTURE CREDITS

Justine Blau is a screenwriter and journalist whose articles have appeared in *Rolling Stone,* the *Village Voice,* and *Newsday.* She is currently enrolled in the graduate screenwriting/directing program at Columbia University Film School. She lives in New York City with her husband and young son.

❖   ❖   ❖

Matina S. Horner is president emerita of Radcliffe College and associate professor of psychology and social relations at Harvard University. She is best known for her studies of women's motivation, achievement, and personality development. Dr. Horner serves on several national boards and advisory councils, including those of the National Science Foundation, Time Inc., and the Women's Research and Education Institute. She earned her B.A. from Bryn Mawr College and Ph.D. from the University of Michigan, and holds honorary degrees from many colleges and universities, including Mount Holyoke, Smith, Tufts, and the University of Pennsylvania.

jB   Blau, Justine
FRIEDAN
            Betty Friedan

$17.95

DATE			

FEB 2 1 1991

SOUTH HUNTINGTON
PUBLIC LIBRARY
2 MELVILLE ROAD
HUNTINGTON STATION, N.Y. 11746

© THE BAKER & TAYLOR CO.